HUMMINGBIRD
GARDENS

Turning Your Yard
Into Hummingbird Heaven

Stephen W. Kress Guest Editor

Steve Buchanan Illustrator

Cover: Sweet, fragrant flowers are irresistable to this Ruby-throated Hummingbird. Title page: Anna's Hummingbirds often perch to sing.

Hummingbird Gardens:
Turning Your Yard into Hummingbird Heaven

Janet Marinelli
SERIES EDITOR

Beth Hanson
CONSULTING EDITOR

Mark Tebbitt
SCIENCE EDITOR

Anne Garland
ART DIRECTOR

Brooklyn Botanic Garden

Elizabeth Peters
DIRECTOR OF PUBLICATIONS

Sigrun Wolff Saphire
SENIOR EDITOR

Joni Blackburn
COPY EDITOR

Steven Clemants
VICE-PRESIDENT, SCIENCE & PUBLICATIONS

Scot Medbury
PRESIDENT

Judith D. Zuk
PRESIDENT EMERITUS

Elizabeth Scholtz
DIRECTOR EMERITUS

HANDBOOK #163

Copyright © 2000, 2007 (revised edition) by Brooklyn Botanic Garden, Inc.
Handbooks in the *21st-Century Gardening Series* (now *All-Region Guides*)
are published at 1000 Washington Ave., Brooklyn, NY 11225.
Subscription included in Brooklyn Botanic Garden subscriber membership dues
($35 per year; $45 outside the United States).
ISBN 13: 978-1-889538-33-4 ISBN 10: 1-889538-33-7
Printed by OGP in China. Printed on recycled paper.

TABLE OF CONTENTS

The Magnificent Hummingbird (*Eugenes fulgens*) derives its species name from the Latin "*fulgere*," meaning to gleam or glitter.

"Glittering Garments of the Rainbow"

by Stephen W. Kress

NEARLY EVERYTHING ABOUT HUMMINGBIRDS is superlative. The common names of many hummers—Ruby-throated, Amethyst-throated, Garnet-throated, Berylline, Crimson-Topaz, and Emerald-chinned—bring to mind their exquisite, gemlike qualities. These tiniest of all vertebrates also have (relative to body size) the largest flight muscles, the biggest brain, the fastest wingbeat, the most rapid heartbeat, the highest body temperature, the greatest appetite, and the most prodigious thirst. Their stamina is so great that they can migrate thousands of miles each year—including hundreds of miles nonstop over water.

Their incessant travels often take hummingbirds to backyard gardens, where they and their insect counterparts, butterflies, congregate. As entrancing as butterflies, hummers dash from one tempting bloom to the next with remarkable energy and agility. It's little wonder that many gardeners are adding hummingbird-attracting blossoms to existing gardens or creating special plantings to lure these feisty visitors. Hummingbirds occasionally visit most gardens, but they only stay when they find special flowers that provide ample food. This handbook explains how you can entice hummingbirds to visit your garden and get them to linger there, enlivening the floral displays with their glittering colors and bold, inquisitive personalities.

The Black-chinned Hummingbird sports an iridescent-purple throat.

If you have already graced your yard with plants attractive to butterflies, you will find that gardening for hummingbirds is in many ways similar. For example, both hummingbirds and butterflies share similar tastes in some flowers, such as butterfly weed and gayfeathers. However, one notable difference is that hummingbird flowers are typically red, tube-shaped, and without scent, while butterfly flowers are more varied in color and almost always heavily perfumed.

Throughout their long migrations, hummingbirds are vulnerable to weather, disease, and predators. Like other migrants, hummingbirds are also susceptible to habitat loss, pesticides, and collisions with windows, tall buildings, towers, and power lines. There isn't much that gardeners can do to increase the chances of survival of many species of birds, such as those who live deep in forest interiors. By contrast, hummingbirds do profit from backyard plantings where they can find meals of nectar and insects, as well as the sugar water in feeders that sprout from an increasing number of porches and kitchen windows each spring.

Too often, human activities worsen the plight of birds and other wildlife by polluting or destroying their habitats, or through the planting of invasive species that overrun the native vegetation with which wildlife has coevolved. By planting the native wildflowers upon which North American hummingbirds have depended for thousands of years, you will not only bring vibrant color to your garden, but you will also insure a brighter future for the birds that John James Audubon called "glittering garments of the rainbow."

Lifestyles of the Nectar Sippers

by Stephen W. Kress

HUMMINGBIRDS ARE UNIQUE TO THE AMERICAS. The vast majority of the 340 species of hummingbirds occur in the tropics. Twenty-two species are found in the United States, most of them in the Southwest. Only one species, the Ruby-throated Hummingbird, nests in the eastern states and Canadian provinces.

HUMMINGBIRD MIGRATION

While most hummingbirds are nonmigratory or short-distance migrants, there are two notable exceptions. The Rufous Hummingbird migrates from its winter home in Mexico as far north as southern Alaska. Remarkably, many Ruby-throated Hummingbirds migrate more than 600 miles across the Gulf of Mexico, making landfall in the southeastern states. After crossing the border, some continue north, while others move eastward, reoccupying nesting habitat in all the eastern states and Canadian provinces.

NECTAR SIPPING

The appearance of migrating hummingbirds in spring may be timed to the appearance of nectar-producing wildflowers—or perhaps the flowers time their blooming to the arrival of the hummingbirds! For example, arrival of the Ruby-throated Hummingbird in the northern reaches of its range, where it nests, coincides with the flowering of certain nectar plants, such as wild columbine (*Aquilegia canadensis*), as well as with the arrival of migrating Yellow-bellied Sapsuckers, which drill "sap wells" in trees from which hummingbirds readily feed. The migration of hummers of the western mountains also coincides with the flowering of favorite nectar plants. (However, hummingbirds' southern migration in autumn is triggered by changes in day length, not by the scarcity of nectar plants, which are still abundant.)

Many birds, including orioles and at least 50 other species, have an appetite for sugar water and tree sap, but hummers are the ultimate nectar specialists. This high-energy diet provides fuel for flight speeds of 40 miles per hour (66 miles per hour—and up to 200 wing strokes per second—during courtship). Ruby-throated Hummingbirds typically weigh less than 4 grams (females slightly more), but their body weight can double in a week as they fatten on nectar, as well as insects and spiders, before beginning their fall migration.

FLEXIBLE FLYING

Hummingbirds are the only birds that can fly up, down, sideways, and even backward, a talent that enables them to easily sip nectar from flowers and pluck invertebrates out of thin air. Such extraordinary flight is due in part to their relatively huge breast muscles, which compose up to 30 percent of their total weight—the highest proportion of any bird.

Their fast-paced foraging style permits hummingbirds to hover where there are no convenient perches—for instance, at the entrance to swaying flower stems, where they feed in place. This unique hovering ability permits them to feed on as many as 1,500 flowers each day; they may drink twice their weight in sugar water daily. Their skill at backward flight allows them to back off to look over the banquet scene before charging forward for refueling.

BODY HEAT

Relative to body size, hummers have the largest heart of all warm-blooded animals, with the fastest heartbeat—1,260 beats each minute. Their daytime body temperature reaches 105°F. They are the only birds that regularly become torpid at night, when their temperature plummets from daytime levels.

Hummingbirds and their favorite flowers have coevolved over the millennia. The birds use their long bills to probe for nectar at the base of tubular blooms.

HUMMINGBIRD IQ

Although hummingbirds are curious and are often attracted to bright red colors on objects that have little resemblance to flowers (such as colorful clothing and red stripes on flags), they quickly learn which red objects provide productive treats. They also have remarkable memories and can recall from one year to the next the location of a particularly rich nectar patch or reliable hummingbird feeder. Observations of partially albino birds (which have unique color patterns) have demonstrated that individual hummingbirds often return to the same backyard over several consecutive years, which may be most of their relatively short lives.

FITTING THE BILL

Hummingbirds and their favorite flowers have clearly coevolved for mutual benefit. Most hummingbird flowers share a similar shape, regardless of their family affinities. Look for tubular flowers with stamens and pistil often dangling from the flower's entrance. The typical flower shape protects a nectar bait that encourages this long-billed bird to probe deeply for its sweet meal. In the process, the bird picks up pollen on its crown, and the pollen is then transferred to the next flower from which it feeds. Some hummingbirds have learned to "steal" nectar by piercing the side of the flower without picking up pollen, but plants such as bird-of-paradise and other heliconias have evolved to counter this behavior with a thickened calyx that discourages nectar thieves.

Many hummingbird-pollinated plants have red or orange flowers, colors that are readily seen by hummingbirds. Unlike insect-pollinated flowers, these blooms are usually not fragrantly perfumed, because hummingbirds (like most birds) have a poorly developed sense of smell.

BUSIER THAN BEES

Compared to insect pollinators such as bees, hummingbirds offer distinct advantages as cross-pollinators. Bees are inactive in cool, wet weather and visit flowers only during the warmer part of the day when their wing mus-

While many birds have an appetite for sugar water and tree sap, hummingbirds are the ultimate flower nectar specialists.

cles have adequately warmed for flight. Hummingbirds are generally better pollinators than bees because they must feed continuously from dawn to dusk. In addition, bees' activities are more confined to fields and forest edges; they seldom visit forest interiors as hummingbirds do. One study that compared the pollinating efficiency of Ruby-throated Hummingbirds and bumblebees found that hummingbirds deposited ten times as much pollen (per stigma per visit) onto the flowers

Ruby-throated Hummingbirds, like this couple, may transfer ten times as much pollen as bumblebees.

of the trumpet creeper, *Campsis radicans*. Another study found that closely related species like the bee balms *Monarda didyma* and *M. clinopodia* may avoid hybridization because particular hummingbird species show preferences for certain nectar flavors and pollen is placed on the hummers in slightly different locations.

COURTSHIP RITUALS

The hummingbird nesting season begins when the male establishes a courtship territory. When a female enters the territory, the male performs a courtship flight unique to his species. In Ruby-throated Hummingbirds, this is a looping, U-shaped flight performed as high as 36 to 45 feet above the female. If impressed by the skill of his flight, the female lands near the male, encouraging him to shift the performance to a series of very fast, side-to-side horizontal arcs, which he performs (with throat gorget extended) within one to two feet of the female. Mating soon follows the courtship performance.

Female hummers, like this shy Allen's, often camouflage their nests with lichens.

NESTING

Females build their nests by themselves on a shrub or tree branch, using mainly thistle and dandelion down. The nest is secured to the branch with spider web and pine resin; its exterior is sometimes camouflaged with lichens, held in place by sticky spider web. Construction takes six to ten days, and during this time, the male continues courting additional mates. Females sometimes refurbish old nests for a second brood, or they may build another nest for their second brood while still feeding the first brood.

A female usually lays two tiny white eggs and incubates them for 12 to 14 days. She broods the young almost constantly until they are nine days old, leaving her nest and young only to obtain food for herself and her brood. Nestlings are fully feathered and capable of flight when they are 18 to 20 days old.

PREDATORS

Hummingbirds have few predators, but shrikes, American kestrels, and sharp-shinned hawks sometimes take adults, and blue jays will take eggs. Attacks by praying mantises, dragonflies, and bullfrogs have also been documented, and hummingbirds are sometimes accidentally entangled in spiderwebs . House cats are probably the most common predators, and collisions with windows, cars, and radio towers are believed to take a huge toll on hummingbird populations.

HUMMINGBIRDS OF NORTH AMERICA

by Lynn Hassler Kaufman

THIS ENCYCLOPEDIA INCLUDES the 18 species of hummingbirds found in the United States and Canada, as well as four "accidentals"—species that are very rarely seen this far north. The encyclopedia entry for each bird includes information on its native range, preferred habitats, and nesting habits, as well as tips to aid in identification. Please note that the hummingbird illustrations are not drawn to scale; see the information in each entry on length (measured from tip of bill to tip of tail) for the accurate size of each species. See the Encyclopedia of Hummingbird Plants, beginning on page 49, for detailed descriptions of hummingbird-attracting flowers for every region.

ALLEN'S HUMMINGBIRD

Selasphorus sasin

Allen's Hummingbird is one of the two common nesting hummingbirds in northern California gardens. The genus name *Selasphorus* means "flame bearing" in Latin. Allen's like to feed on red tubular flowers such as penstemon, monkeyflower, and paintbrush.

RANGE Nests from southwestern Oregon to southwestern California; winters in Mexico. A nonmigratory race resides on the Channel Islands and Palos Verdes Peninsula in southern California.

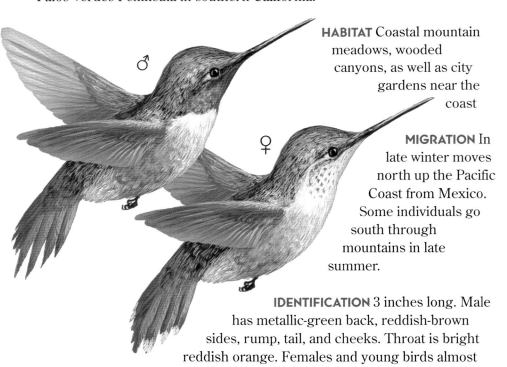

HABITAT Coastal mountain meadows, wooded canyons, as well as city gardens near the coast

MIGRATION In late winter moves north up the Pacific Coast from Mexico. Some individuals go south through mountains in late summer.

IDENTIFICATION 3 inches long. Male has metallic-green back, reddish-brown sides, rump, tail, and cheeks. Throat is bright reddish orange. Females and young birds almost impossible to separate from Rufous Hummingbird in the field.

NESTING HABITS Nests in tree or shrub on horizontal or diagonal branch up to 90 feet above the ground. Sometimes nests in pines or even in buildings; usually in dense shade.

ANNA'S HUMMINGBIRD

Calypte anna

More vocal than most hummers, the male Anna's has a rather unmelodic song: a series of repetitive scratchy notes, often delivered while perched. In winter Anna's Hummingbird often feeds at eucalyptus and tree tobacco flowers.

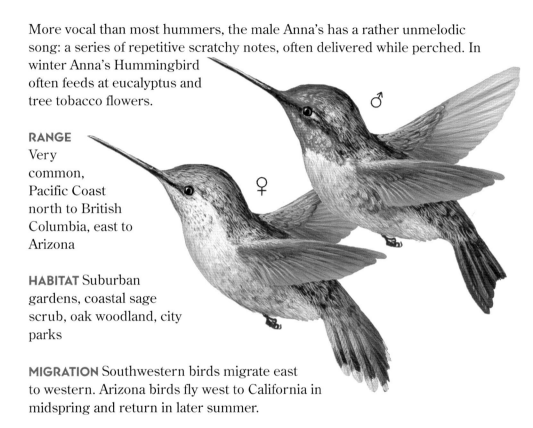

RANGE Very common, Pacific Coast north to British Columbia, east to Arizona

HABITAT Suburban gardens, coastal sage scrub, oak woodland, city parks

MIGRATION Southwestern birds migrate east to western. Arizona birds fly west to California in midspring and return in later summer.

IDENTIFICATION 4 inches long; chunky with bright metallic-green back and gray underparts. Male has a rose-red crown and throat. Females are plainer but usually show a small patch of color on the throat.

NESTING HABITS Some birds begin nesting in December; sites include branches of shrubs and trees (often in oaks), 17 to 30 feet up. Female builds nest out of plant fibers and spiderwebs, often camouflaged on the outside with lichen.

BERYLLINE HUMMINGBIRD

Amazilia beryllina

This hummingbird has been a rare but regular visitor to the U.S. since 1964. When it does show up, it tends to stick around for several months at a time. The Berylline Hummingbird feeds at thistles and will frequent feeders. Its three-noted song sounds like a tiny trumpet.

RANGE Uplands of Mexico; regular visitor in summer to mountains of southeastern Arizona

HABITAT Shady canyons, among sycamores, or in open pine-oak woodland in Arizona, at 5,000 to 7,000 feet; foothills and lower slopes of mountains in Mexico, especially in oak woodland

MIGRATION Probably not migratory over most of its range. In parts of Mexico may move to lower elevations for winter. In summer strays north into southwestern U.S.

IDENTIFICATION 4 inches long; sexes similar. Head and body mostly glittering green, rufous in wings, rump, and tail. Bill black with some red. Female slightly duller, with gray belly.

NESTING HABITS 17 to 25 feet above ground on horizontal branch. In Arizona usually nests in sycamores.

BLACK-CHINNED HUMMINGBIRD

Archilochus alexandri

This species is named for the male, which has a black chin or throat. Black-chinned Hummingbirds often repeatedly flick their tails while hovering over flowers.

RANGE Widespread at low elevations in the West; summers from British Columbia to central Texas and southern California, winters in Mexico.

HABITAT Semi-open arid lowlands, suburbs, open woods, parks, gardens, riparian woodland

MIGRATION Strictly migratory. Arrives in western U.S. in spring and leaves for Mexico in fall. Small numbers may stray east in fall, and a few may winter near the Gulf Coast.

IDENTIFICATION 3 inches long; underparts whitish. Male is bright metallic green above and has a black throat with white collar below. In certain lights the throat shows an iridescent purple border. Females and young birds may have dusky streaks on throat.

NESTING HABITS Usually nests on a horizontal or diagonal branch in a deciduous tree or shrub 4 to 8 feet up. Often nests in backyards and gardens.

BLUE-THROATED HUMMINGBIRD

Lampornis clemenciae

These hummingbirds are the largest of the U.S.-breeding species, the size of some sparrows. As they approach other hummers at flowers or feeders, they aggressively flash their striking black and white tails. Blue-throated Hummingbirds like shady spots near water. Their call note is a squeaky "seek," often delivered in flight.

♂

♀

RANGE Southwestern U.S. to southern Mexico

HABITAT Wooded streams in lower mountain canyons, sycamores, pine-oak woodland, coniferous forest

MIGRATION Most U.S. birds depart in fall; probably resident over most of its range in Mexico.

IDENTIFICATION 5 inches long. Green above, large black tail with white corners, two white face stripes. Male has light blue throat, often difficult to see, and gray underparts. Female's throat is gray.

NESTING HABITS Usually streamside on branch sheltered by overhanging limb, sometimes on exposed root on undercut streambank or under building eaves, 1 to 30 feet up. Outer covering of nest is green moss, unique among North American hummer nests.

BROAD-BILLED HUMMINGBIRD

Cynanthus latirostris

Broad-billed Hummingbirds have a limited range in the U.S. but are abundant where found. Their distinctive voice is a series of dry, crackling notes.

RANGE March to September in limited areas of Arizona, New Mexico, and southwestern Texas; winters in Mexico.

HABITAT Desert canyons, low oak woodlands, foothills, streamsides with sycamores or cottonwoods, mesquite thickets

MIGRATION Nests spring through summer in the Southwest; migrates south into Mexico in the fall. Small numbers may overwinter in Arizona and southern California.

IDENTIFICATION 4 inches long; male glistens all over with iridescent feathers of green and blue, including metallic blue throat; reddish-orange bill; forked tail is blackish blue. Female has grayish underparts, eye stripe, reddish bill, and blackish-blue tail.

NESTING HABITS Deciduous shrub, vine, or low branch on tree 3 to 9 feet above ground. Unlike most other North American hummers, does not usually use lichen on outside of nest.

BROAD-TAILED HUMMINGBIRD

Selasphorus platycercus

This is the classic hummingbird of the mountain West. Adult males create high-pitched trilling sounds with certain wing feathers while flying.

RANGE Breeds in southern and central Rockies and mountains of the Great Basin south into Texas and Mexico; winters in Mexico to Guatemala.

HABITAT Mountain meadows and forests to over 10,000 feet

MIGRATION Adult males usually migrate before females and young. Broad-tailed Hummingbirds tend to fly northward through lowlands in the spring and south through the mountains in late summer.

IDENTIFICATION
4 inches long; males have bronze-green backs and bright rose-pink throats. Females and young birds are whitish underneath with some reddish brown on flanks and at sides of tail.

NESTING HABITS
Nests 4 to 15 feet up on low horizontal branches of willow, alder, pine, fir, spruce, aspen; sheltered from above by overhanging branch. Males often launch from willow thickets in mountain meadows for their display flights.

BUFF-BELLIED HUMMINGBIRD

Amazilia yucatanensis

Buff-bellied Hummingbirds are part of the tropical element in southern Texas, often seen visiting flowers such as Turk's-cap lilies, red salvia, and red yucca.

RANGE Mexico, Belize, and Guatemala; mostly summer resident in southern Texas

HABITAT Woodland edges, areas of brush and scattered trees, suburban neighborhoods, especially those with extensive gardens

MIGRATION Relatively common in southern Texas in summer; some individuals remain through the winter. A few move north along Gulf Coast in fall and winter to upper Texas coast and Louisiana.

IDENTIFICATION 4 inches long; bronzy-green back with chestnut tail; throat and breast shiny emerald green; lower breast and belly cinnamon buff. Both sexes look similar.

NESTING HABITS Usually nests in large shrub or small tree such as hackberry, Texas ebony, or cordia. Nest is low, 3 to 10 feet off ground on horizontal or drooping branch or in fork of twig. May refurbish or build on top of old nests.

CALLIOPE HUMMINGBIRD

Stellula calliope

This tiny bird is the smallest in North America. Despite its small size, it is able to survive cold summer nights at high elevations in the Rockies. It is the only U.S. hummer with such a distinctive throat patch. *Stellula* in Latin means "little star."

RANGE Summers in mountains of western North America from southwestern Canada to Baja; winters in Mexico.

HABITAT High mountain forests and meadows; pine-oak woods in Mexico

MIGRATION Migrates northwest in early spring through Pacific lowlands, southeast in late summer, mostly through Rocky Mountain region.

IDENTIFICATION 3 inches long; short bill and tail. Male green above, white below, greenish sides. Reddish purple on throat forms streaks. Female green above, underside tinged with buff; throat lightly spotted.

NESTING HABITS Nests at 10,000 to 11,500 feet. Site is on twig or branch under overhanging foliage, usually 6 to 40 feet up. Sometimes builds on base of old pine cone, making nest look like part of the cone.

COSTA'S HUMMINGBIRD

Calypte costae

The male Costa's Hummingbird performs a daring aerial courtship display. He rises high in the air, often 100 feet or more, and then plunges downward, making a shrill continuous whistle. At the bottom of his dive, he pulls up sharply and flies upward again.

RANGE Deserts of southwestern U.S. (mainly Arizona and California) and northwestern Mexico

HABITAT Desert washes, sage scrub, lower parts of dry canyons among cacti, yucca, and ocotillo

MIGRATION Many of the birds that nest in the desert in spring migrate west to the coast for other seasons.

IDENTIFICATION 3 inches long; male has iridescent violet crown and violet throat color that sweeps back to a sharp point and flares out on either side of his neck. Female has a green back; crown often dull brown; dingy white below.

NESTING HABITS Nests in open spots with good visibility, sparsely leafed shrubs or small trees, 2 to 8 feet up; often in yucca. In some areas has adapted to nesting in suburbs.

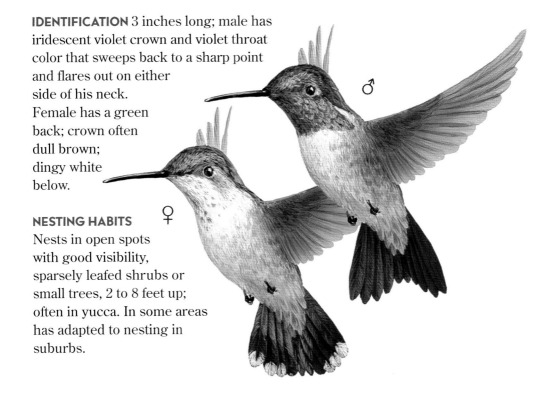

GREEN VIOLETEAR

Colibri thalassinus

This hummingbird is widespread in the mountains of the tropics. Males often perch high in trees and endlessly sing a monotonous series of dry notes. One or two wander into Texas almost every year, and the species has strayed as far east as North Carolina and as far north as Canada.

RANGE Highlands of Mexico, south to Bolivia

HABITAT Oak woods and clearings; forest edges

MIGRATION Nomadic; does not have known regular migration, but ranges far and wide.

IDENTIFICATION 4 inches long; appears dark green overall. Bill slightly downward curving. Male has violet-blue ear patches and breast. Female similar but duller; breast patch smaller or absent.

NESTING HABITS Builds down and ♂ moss cup nest, often placed low.

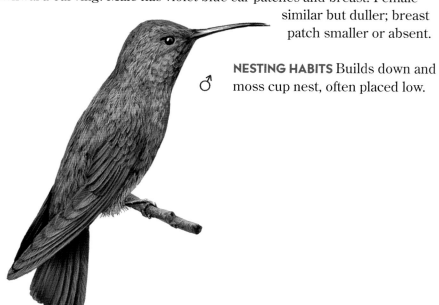

LUCIFER HUMMINGBIRD

Calothorax lucifer

The Lucifer Hummingbird is typical of the Chihuahuan Desert of central Mexico, where it frequents flowering agave stalks and ocotillo. A few reach the southwestern U.S.

RANGE West Texas to southern Mexico; locally in southeastern Arizona and southwestern New Mexico

HABITAT Arid slopes, and desert canyons where agaves grow

MIGRATION Migratory in northern part of range.
Birds from southwestern U.S. and northern Mexico winter in plateaus of south-central Mexico.

IDENTIFICATION 3 inches long; bronze-green back; long decurved bill. Male has dazzling purple throat and sides of neck, buffy sides, and long forked tail that is usually tightly folded. Female's breast uniformly buff colored; pale streak behind eye.

NESTING HABITS Male has a unique courtship display performed in front of female at her nest. Makes short flights back and forth with loud rustling sound of wings, then flies high and dives steeply past the nest. Nests in open cholla cactus or on ocotillo stem or agave stalk, 2 to 10 feet up.

MAGNIFICENT HUMMINGBIRD

Eugenes fulgens

At a distance, this very large hummingbird looks all black. Its wingbeats are slower than those of smaller hummingbirds and are actually discernible in flight. The species name is from the Latin *fulgere*, meaning "to gleam or glitter." Formerly called Rivoli's Hummingbird.

RANGE Southwestern U.S to Panama; strays have been seen as far north as Minnesota.

HABITAT Pine-oak woodlands, canyons with sycamore, and coniferous forests in higher mountains, 5,000 to 9,000 feet

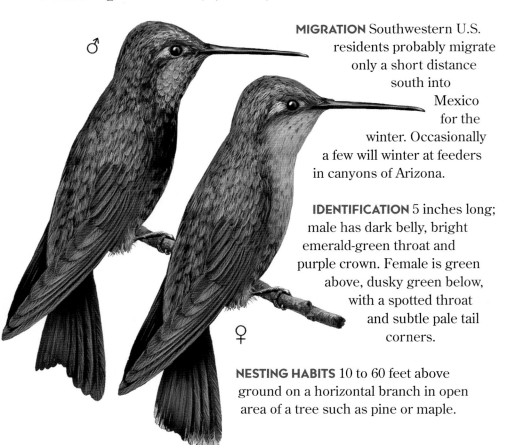

MIGRATION Southwestern U.S. residents probably migrate only a short distance south into Mexico for the winter. Occasionally a few will winter at feeders in canyons of Arizona.

IDENTIFICATION 5 inches long; male has dark belly, bright emerald-green throat and purple crown. Female is green above, dusky green below, with a spotted throat and subtle pale tail corners.

NESTING HABITS 10 to 60 feet above ground on a horizontal branch in open area of a tree such as pine or maple.

RUBY-THROATED HUMMINGBIRD

Archilochus colubris

The Ruby-throated Hummingbird is the only hummer found regularly east of the Great Plains. In its northern distribution it often feeds on tree sap provided by the drilling of sapsuckers. It is especially attracted to flowers of bee balms (*Monarda* species), trumpet creeper (*Campsis radicans*), columbines (*Aquilegia* species), and red salvias (*Salvia* species).

RANGE Southeastern Canada to Gulf Coast states; winters in southern Texas, southern Florida to western Panama.

HABITAT Gardens, woodland edges, city parks; winters in open or dry tropical scrub.

MIGRATION Many migrate around the Gulf of Mexico, but others may fly across it—600 miles over open water.

IDENTIFICATION 3 inches long; iridescent green back, forked tail. Undersides whitish, sides and flanks dusky green. Male has a fiery red throat. Female throat whitish, grayish white below with slightly buffy sides.

NESTING HABITS On horizontal branch or one that slopes downward in hemlock or deciduous tree such as maple or beech; also in large shrubs. May reuse old nests.

RUFOUS HUMMINGBIRD

Selasphorus rufus

Feisty and aggressive, Rufous Hummingbirds defend patches of flowers or feeders, driving away other birds that attempt to approach. This bird is a champion long-distance migrant, wintering in Mexico and nesting as far north as Alaska—farther north than any other hummer.

RANGE Pacific Northwest to south-central Alaska; winters in Mexico; small numbers winter in Gulf Coast states.

HABITAT Forest edges and clearings, streamsides

MIGRATION In spring moves northward through Pacific lowlands. Beginning in late June, moves southeast through Rocky Mountains and Sierra, following seasonal blooming of flowers.

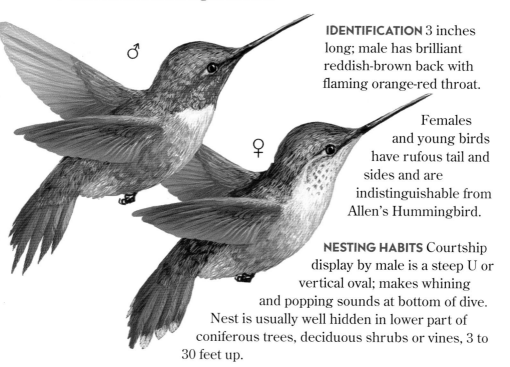

IDENTIFICATION 3 inches long; male has brilliant reddish-brown back with flaming orange-red throat.

Females and young birds have rufous tail and sides and are indistinguishable from Allen's Hummingbird.

NESTING HABITS Courtship display by male is a steep U or vertical oval; makes whining and popping sounds at bottom of dive. Nest is usually well hidden in lower part of coniferous trees, deciduous shrubs or vines, 3 to 30 feet up.

PLAIN-CAPPED STARTHROAT

Heliomaster constantii

This large, drab hummingbird is a rare visitor to southern Arizona. In its native habitat it is often seen hovering over rivers catching insects.

RANGE Mexico and Central America

HABITAT Dry thorn forests; in Arizona has been found in lowland areas near streams or open, lower parts of canyons

MIGRATION Probably doesn't migrate within permanent range; has reached Arizona mostly in summer and fall.

IDENTIFICATION 4 inches long; overall looks quite dull; long billed. Male has red throat, but color is quite difficult to see; white stripes on face; white rump and tufts on flanks.

NESTING HABITS Cup-shaped nest in branches of trees and shrubs.

VIOLET-CROWNED HUMMINGBIRD

Amazilia violiceps

This hummingbird only recently arrived in the U.S. It was unknown north of the border until the late 1950s and is still quite scarce and localized. Where flowers are not abundant, it can be seen hovering mid-level in the shade of tall trees, catching insects.

RANGE Mainly western Mexico; regular in summer in a few places in southeastern Arizona and southwestern New Mexico

HABITAT Arid or semiarid open woodland; in U.S. mostly near groves of tall trees (especially sycamores and cottonwoods) with brushy understory

MIGRATION Probably permanent resident over most of range; seen mostly in summer in U.S.

IDENTIFICATION 4 inches long; sexes similar; bright white underparts, including the throat. Bill bright red, tipped with black. Upperpart bronzy green, tail greenish; violet-blue crown (duller in female).

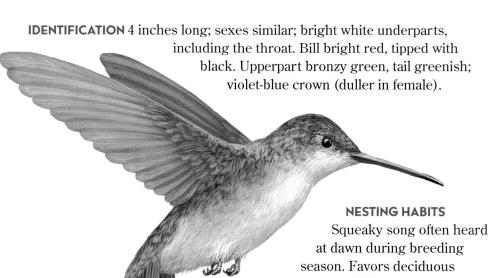

NESTING HABITS
Squeaky song often heard at dawn during breeding season. Favors deciduous trees, especially sycamore, or large shrubs in open but shaded spot 4 to 40 feet up.

WHITE-EARED HUMMINGBIRD

Hylocharis leucotis

This Mexican species is a regular but uncommon visitor to the mountain forests of southeastern Arizona.

RANGE Mexican border to Nicaragua; a few reach southwestern U.S.

HABITATS In Mexico, high mountain forests; in clearings and edges of coniferous forests; pine-oak woods at middle elevations. In southern Arizona, most are seen in mountain canyons where feeders are maintained.

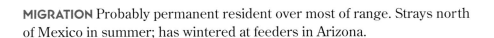

MIGRATION Probably permanent resident over most of range. Strays north of Mexico in summer; has wintered at feeders in Arizona.

IDENTIFICATION 3 inches long; sports a bright red bill tipped with black; blackish-blue forked tail, long white stripe behind eye. Male has blue and green throat and purple crown. Female has white stripe behind eye and small green spots on throat.

NESTING HABITS Males gather in loose groups, perch 60 to 100 feet apart, and sing short songs to attract females. Nest site is 5 to 20 feet above ground on a twig or in fork of shrub or tree.

Rare Visitors

The following "accidental" species are very rare visitors to the United States.

GREEN-BREASTED MANGO

Anthracothorax prevostii

This large, bulky hummer with a slightly curved bill is widespread in the lowlands of the American tropics around forest edges and clearings. It has wandered to southern Texas a few times. Male is all green (blacker on throat) with a magenta tail. Female has a wide black stripe down the center of the white breast.

BAHAMA WOODSTAR

Green-breasted Mango

Calliphlox evelynae

Though native to islands in the Bahamas, this hummer occasionally wanders to southern Florida. The male is green above with a deeply forked black-and-buff tail. A white upper-breast band, like a partial collar, contrasts with the cinnamon belly and purple throat. The female has a white throat and unforked tail.

XANTUS'S HUMMINGBIRD

Hylocharis xantusii

This Mexican hummer of the southern half of Baja California likes mountain canyons, especially with water. It has been found very rarely in southern California and once in British Columbia. The male has an emerald-green

throat, black-tipped reddish bill, and a white stripe behind the eye. The underparts are mainly buff, and the tail is chestnut colored. The female is all buff below, with chestnut in the tail.

CINNAMON HUMMINGBIRD

Amazilia rutila

This common, colorful hummer of arid scrub and brushy forest edges in western and southern Mexico was not recorded in the U.S. until 1992, when one was found in southern Ari-

Above: Xantus's Hummingbird
Below: Cinnamon Hummingbird

zona. Both sexes have green backs and bright cinnamon underparts. The tail is rufous, and the bill is red tipped with black.

Hummingbird Moths: Marvelous Masqueraders

by Stephen W. Kress

HUMMINGBIRD GARDENS ARE IDEAL PLACES to watch for hummer look-alikes—the hummingbird moths. In a classic example of convergent evolution, these stout-bodied insects with swept-back wings dine on flower nectar and pollinate flowers in a manner remarkably similar to hummingbirds. Like their avian namesakes, they can hover in place while tapping nectar reserves with their long, uncoiled tongues. Some species even have green backs, further adding to their hummingbird resemblance. Unlike hummingbirds, though, they are late risers, waiting until the sun warms their wing muscles and stirs them into action.

Members of the sphinx moth family, this enormously varied group derives its family name from the caterpillars that can pull their forebody up into a sphinxlike pose. The caterpillars are known as hornworms because they have a long, harmless spine that arises menacingly from their back near their posterior. While most sphinx moths visit flowers at night, hummingbird moths (also called clearwings because of the transparent patches in their wings) frequent gardens in full daylight. At a distance, some black and yellow species resemble huge bumblebees; however, bees settle on the flower, descending into the bloom, while hummingbird moths feed in a tireless manner, seldom resting.

Hummingbird-moth caterpillars feed mainly on honeysuckle, hawthorn, snowberry, and viburnum, but different species have special taste preferences. The caterpillars transform into pupae, which are enclosed in well-hidden, dense brown cocoons formed on the ground under fallen leaves. Some pupae overwinter under leaves, leaving their cocoons as flying adults

Hummingbird moths, like their avian namesakes, can hover in place as they drink flower nectar with their long, uncoiled tongues.

the following spring. Double- or triple-brooded species pass through the pupal stage in midsummer, emerging as adults in late summer and fall.

Taxonomists have struggled with this group, since moths of the same species often vary in appearance depending on their location, and sometimes they vary even between broods in the same location. It is now generally agreed, however, that there are four species of hummingbird moths in North America. Range can help to sort them out, but several species overlap and at first glance are hard to distinguish. All species have clear parts in their wings, and the males have a dramatic anal tuft, often in varied colors. In northern climates, hummingbird moths appear in midsummer, while those in southern climates often have two broods, the first in midspring, the second in midsummer into late fall.

Hummingbird moth gardeners don't have to plant special flowers to attract the adults, but the larvae do require specific shrubs for food (see species descriptions on following pages).

COMMON CLEARWING

Hemaris thysbe

This is the largest and most common of the hummingbird moths. Although there is considerable variation, the abdomen is marked with narrow or broad bands. The thorax is generally a uniform muddy yellow or solid brown. Like those of other hummingbird moths, the forewings have clear cells edged with black. Males have a distinctive black tuft at the tip of their abdomen.

RANGE Newfoundland to Florida, across to Texas, north along the eastern Great Plains, west to southern British Columbia, north to southern Alaska

SEASONS In the north, this species has one brood and adults emerge in midsummer. In the South, where two broods are produced, adults visit gardens from March to June and again from August to October.

CATERPILLAR FOODS Hawthorns (*Crataegus* species), cherries and plums (*Prunus* species), honeysuckles (*Lonicera* species), and snowberry (*Symphoricarpos* species)

GRACEFUL CLEARWING

Hemaris gracilis

This is the least common of the four hummingbird moth species, but it may be locally abundant, especially in the mid-Atlantic states. It closely resembles the common clearwing but is easily distinguished by the pair of red-brown bands on the sides of its thorax. The thorax varies from green to yellow-green and sometimes brown. The underside of the thorax is white. The abdomen is pale red with three rows of white spots on the underside. The anal tuft is black, divided in the middle with reddish hairs. Specimens from South Carolina and Florida are usually dark brown.

RANGE Nova Scotia to central Florida along the East Coast and west through the New England states to Michigan

SEASONS In the northern part of its range, it may have two broods or have a long emergence period. Adults start feeding at flowers in Nova Scotia from early June to early August; Michigan from the end of May through early July; New York in mid-May and July; South Carolina in April; and central Florida in late March.

CATERPILLAR FOODS
Unknown

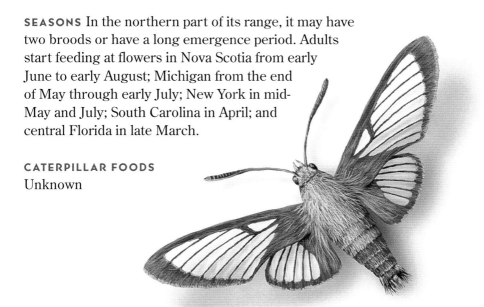

SNOWBERRY CLEARWING

Hemaris diffinis

This is a variable species, with more black markings on the thorax, abdomen, and legs than other clearwings.

RANGE Nova Scotia to Florida across to California and north to British Columbia and the Northwest Territories

SEASONS This species has two broods throughout most of its range. Adults begin visiting flowers from spring into midsummer.

CATERPILLAR FOODS Various species of dogbane (*Apocynum*), dwarf bush honeysuckle (*Diervilla lonicera*), snowberries (*Symphoricarpos* species) and honeysuckles (*Lonicera* species)

CALIFORNIA CLEARWING

Hemaris senta

The head, thorax, and basal segments of the abdomen are brownish olive or olive-green. The abdomen is black or olive-green above and yellow below, except for a broad yellow band just above the terminal segment of the abdomen. The anal tuft is completely black. The wings have a very narrow border of brown, and the clear parts of the wings have a steel-blue luster in certain lights. Sometimes the wings are pale rusty red above and below where they join the thorax.

RANGE New Mexico, Colorado, Utah, Wyoming, west to California and British Columbia

SEASONS Adults are on the wing May to mid-August.

CATERPILLAR FOODS Unknown

Designing a Hummingbird Garden
15 Ways to
Keep Them Coming

by Stephen W. Kress

HUMMINGBIRDS PREFER CLEARINGS in the forest and forest edge, and so are readily drawn to suburban and rural gardens that offer a mix of tall trees, shrubs, and patches of meadow and lawn. They are less likely to frequent cities, perhaps because they find fewer flowering plants for food and trees for nesting. Yet even in the largest cities, hummingbirds occupy parks and sometimes visit window boxes or rooftop gardens planted with bright flowers, especially during migration.

Once hummingbirds discover your property, the same individuals are likely to return each year at about the same time; they are remarkable creatures of habit. The number of hummingbirds that frequent your yard is closely linked to the abundance of food, water, nesting sites, and perches. Following are 15 practical steps you can take to create an ideal hummingbird garden.

STEP 1
Draw a sketch of your yard, indicating the location of the house and outbuildings such as garages and toolsheds. Include trees, shrubs, existing flower beds, and other features likely to benefit hummingbirds. Work with what you already have, enhancing the yard with additional plantings.

Right: Keep in mind that hummingbirds are attracted to red, pink, and orange tubular flowers such as this *Ipomopsis rubra.*

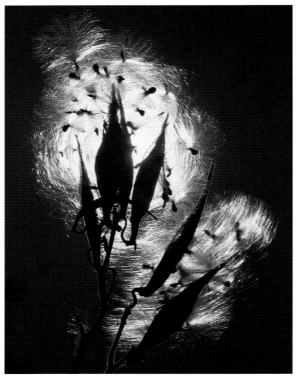

Hummers usually line their nests with soft fibers, so include some fuzzy plants in your garden.

STEP 2

Using your landscape sketch, find a good spot to be the focus of your hummingbird garden. A site near a window or patio door will give you a front seat on the action. Hummingbird gardens need not be large—even a flower box or trellis will do. Gardens planted exclusively with hummingbird plants will attract more birds, but even a few choice plants added to existing gardens will entice hummers.

STEP 3

Think vertically when planning your hummingbird garden. Use trellises, trees, sheds, or other structures to support climbing vines; add window boxes, wooden tubs, or ceramic pots to create a terraced effect and provide growing places for a variety of plants.

STEP 4

Select native plants for your garden. Learn which plants hummingbirds feed on in natural areas near your home. Native hummingbird plants and local hummingbird species have a long association in which plants serve as a reliable source of nectar at the same time each year. Keep in mind that cultivated varieties of impatiens and rhododendrons may look promising but have little value to hummingbirds; these are selected for flower size, color, and shape but are not good nectar producers.

Do not plant exotic flowering plants, such as Japanese and tartarian honeysuckles, which are attractive to hummingbirds but invade neighboring fields and woodlands, crowding out more beneficial native shrubs and wildflowers.

STEP 5
Choose plants with flowers that are red and/or tubular —two qualities that add to a flower's value as a hummingbird food supply. Hummingbirds are also drawn to orange and pink flowers, but they find yellow and white blooms less attractive.

Red, non-tubular flowers such as roses and geraniums may lure hummingbirds to the garden with their blooms, but they offer little nectar, so the birds quickly reject

Hummingbird gardens needn't be large—even a window box or hanging planter will do.

them. Flowers that rely on sweet scents to attract insect pollinators usually do not provide a nectar source for hummingbirds.

STEP 6
Plant patches of the same species (three or more plants) to provide larger quantities of nectar, as well as bigger targets for roving hummers.

STEP 7
Select plants that bloom at different times of the year to provide nectar throughout the hummingbird season.

STEP 8
Prune your plants to prevent excessive woody growth and instead encourage production of flowers.

STEP 9

Learn about local hummingbird habits and which species are likely to occur near your home. Study their migration dates, nesting season, and seasonal presence. This knowledge will help you select plants that will bloom during the time that hummingbirds are likely to visit your yard.

STEP 10

Include some fuzzy plants. Hummingbirds usually line their nest with soft plant fibers. Two favorites are cinnamon fern, which has a fuzzy stem, and pussy willow. Leave some thistle and dandelion, other favorite nest-building materials, in your yard.

STEP 11

Provide water baths. Like most birds, hummingbirds frequently bathe in shallow water—even in the drops that collect on leaves. Hummingbirds may sit and fluff and preen or flit through the droplets generated by garden mis-

The small waterfall and the bright red blooms of bee balm make this garden a more enticing spot for hummingbirds.

ters, drip fountain devices, and small waterfalls; these are available at many garden shops.

STEP 12

If your garden does not include trees or shrubs and there are none nearby, position perches within 10 to 20 feet of the garden. As a substitute for a live perch, use a dead branch with small twigs (keep in mind the tiny size of hummingbird toes).

Hummers are fond of small branches upon which they can perch.

STEP 13

Large trees are often used for perches, as springboards for courtship displays, and for nesting. The trunks of large trees also provide hummingbirds with a source of lichens—a camouflaging decoration that some species attach to the outside of their nest with spider silk. If space permits, plant large trees such as maples or oaks. If you have a smaller yard, plant smaller trees or large shrubs that can provide nest sites and serve as food sources.

STEP 14

Be persistent. Hummingbirds may appear minutes after you set out inviting plants, but sometimes it takes several weeks before they happen upon your garden. Even with luscious red flowers as bait, pure chance may keep your feeder a secret until the first migrant discovers it. Once hummingbirds do start visiting your garden, they are likely to continue throughout the season and will usually return the following year. If visits drop off for a week or two in midsummer, it may be that an especially attractive nearby flower patch has temporarily diverted your hummingbirds.

STEP 15

Avoid using pesticides. Hummingbirds can ingest poisons when they eat insects; systemic herbicides can also be found in flower nectar.

Hummingbird Feeders

by Stephen W. Kress

THE BEST WAY TO FEED HUMMINGBIRDS is to offer them nectar-producing flowers, but hummingbird feeders can act as a supplement and lure birds to spots where you can easily watch them. Hummingbirds are entranced by sugar water in colorful feeders—after all, no flower in nature has such vast amounts of sweet nectar. Yet hummingbird feeders can become hazards to the birds unless they are responsibly tended. Here are a few suggestions:

When you purchase your first hummingbird feeder, choose one with a small reservoir for sugar water. You will have to fill this more frequently, but the sugar-water supply will be fresher. As hummingbirds find your feeder and make it a popular stop, add more feeders or a larger feeder, selecting models that are easy to clean. Feeders with multiple sipping ports and perches can accommodate many birds at once.

Hang the feeder in a shady spot; the sugar water is less likely to spoil there. Keep the feeder within easy view of windows; placing the feeder within a foot or two of a window is usually safe, but move it if humming-birds begin colliding with the glass. Also keep the feeder at least six feet

Ambrosia for Hummingbirds

To prepare a batch of sugar water for a hummingbird feeder, mix one part granulated white sugar to four parts water, then boil the solution for one or two minutes; don't let the brew turn to syrup. Cool the mixture before filling feeders and store the surplus in your refrigerator. Do not use honey, as it ferments easily and promotes fungus growth that can prove harmful. Most feeders have enough red plastic parts to lure the birds, so it isn't necessary to add red food coloring to the sugar water.

Use colorful feeders to lure hummingbirds where you can easily observe them feeding and interacting with each other.

off the ground to reduce the risk from predatory house cats. Place the feeder near a shrub or tree, which can provide convenient perches and shelter—or securely nail a branch with slender branchlets close by to accommodate tiny hummingbird feet.

To attract hummingbirds when you first put up the feeder, dangle colorful plastic or silk flowers from it. Once hummingbirds discover the feeder, they will remember its location.

Refill the feeders as soon as they are empty to keep up a dependable food source. Clean the feeder at least once a week with a bottle brush. Discourage ants by suspending a plastic cup filled with water from the line leading to the feeder. Use special plastic "bee guards" to prevent large insects from clogging the feeder tube.

Feeders do not usually deter hummingbirds from migration. In northern climates, leave feeders in place until the last hummingbirds depart for the winter, then clean and store them for the season. In warm climates, it's okay to use hummingbird feeders throughout the year, especially on the West Coast and in the Southwest. There is growing evidence that many hummingbirds (and many species) winter in the southeastern states, where they feed on flowers, insects, and tree sap released by sapsuckers. Wintering hummingbirds should not be captured, held in greenhouses, or transported to tropical climates.

As hummers, such as this Ruby-throated Hummingbird, sip nectar, they pick up pollen on their crowns. The pollen is transferred to the next flower on which they feed.

ENCYCLOPEDIA
OF HUMMINGBIRD
PLANTS

ON THE FOLLOWING PAGES you will find descriptions of dozens of choice hummingbird-attracting plants for the Northeast and Midwest, Southeast, western mountains and deserts, and the Pacific Coast of the U.S. and Canada. Most of the selected plants are natives that occur naturally within each region, or they are common, noninvasive garden plants. Cultivars and related species are listed only if they are attractive to hummingbirds. In addition to the featured plants for every region, each section includes a list of other good choices, some of which are recommended for adjacent regions. Note the hardiness zones for each selection to help you choose plants that are likely to survive winter conditions in your area. A map of the USDA hardiness zones is on page 106.

Hummingbird Plants for the Northeast and Midwest

by Stephen W. Kress

Aesculus pavia
RED BUCKEYE

NATIVE HABITAT Eastern U.S.

GROWTH TYPE Shrub or small tree

HARDINESS ZONES 5 to 8

FLOWER COLOR Red, sometimes marked with yellow, borne in 6-inch conical clusters in spring

HEIGHT 10 to 25 feet with a spread of 10 feet

BLOOMING PERIOD Late spring to early summer

HOW TO GROW Plant in full sun or partial shade in fertile, moist to wet soils; best to buy trees that are balled and wrapped in burlap or in containers to retain the long tap root. The palmately compound, shiny dark leaves are prone to leaf scorch, leaf blotch, and moths; prune in early spring as necessary.

Agastache cana
HUMMINGBIRD'S MINT, GIANT HYSSOP

NATIVE HABITAT Western Texas

GROWTH TYPE Spreading perennial herb

HARDINESS ZONES 5 to 10

FLOWER COLOR Dark pink to orange flowers

HEIGHT 1 to 2 feet

BLOOMING PERIOD Late summer to autumn

HOW TO GROW Plant in full sun; drought tolerant and easy to maintain

CULTIVARS AND RELATED SPECIES 'Firebird' is a 2- to 6-foot perennial with coppery-red to coral-orange flowers and woody base. *A. barberi*, giant hummingbird's mint, is a 2-foot-tall shrubby perennial with 12-inch spikes of rose to light magenta flowers from midsummer to fall, Zones 6 to 10. *A.* 'Tutti-frutti' is an erect, scented, 2- to 6-foot-tall perennial with raspberry-red flowers on loose spikes from mid-summer to late fall.

Aquilegia canadensis
WILD COLUMBINE

NATIVE HABITAT Forest edges from eastern Canada to Florida
GROWTH TYPE Perennial herb
HARDINESS ZONES 3 to 8
FLOWER COLOR Many nodding red flowers with yellow centers
HEIGHT 1 to 2 feet with a spread of 1 foot
BLOOMING PERIOD Late spring to early summer
HOW TO GROW Partial to full sun; prefers damp soil but will not grow in soggy conditions; protect from wind; cut back old stems for a second crop of flowers; leave seeds to feed juncos and sparrows; plants may need to be replaced every three years.
CULTIVARS AND RELATED SPECIES Cultivated varieties with red or orange flowers are especially attractive to hummingbirds.

Asclepias tuberosa
BUTTERFLY WEED

NATIVE HABITAT Prairies of central and eastern U.S.
GROWTH TYPE Herbaceous annual; typical milkweed shape

Top: *Aquilegia canadensis*
Bottom: *Asclepias tuberosa*

Dicentra eximia

HARDINESS ZONES 4 to 9
FLOWER COLOR Broad clusters of bright orange flowers
HEIGHT 6 inches to 3 feet
BLOOMING PERIOD Early to late summer
HOW TO GROW Well-drained, sandy soils in full sun. Spring growth starts late, so do not overwater or disturb dormant plants.
CULTIVARS AND RELATED SPECIES Most, if not all, species of *Asclepias* attract hummingbirds and insects.
NOTE: Butterflies and hummingbirds obtain nectar from the flowers; hummingbirds also feed on insects that are attracted to the sweet nectar.

Canna species
CANNA, INDIAN SHOT
NATIVE HABITAT Forest borders of Asia and tropical North and South America
GROWTH TYPE Herbaceous, noted for large, paddle-shaped leaves and spectacular flowers
HARDINESS ZONES 8 to 11; grown as annual in the Northeast.
FLOWER COLOR Red, orange, pink, yellow
HEIGHT 2 to 7 feet
BLOOMING PERIOD Midsummer to early autumn
HOW TO GROW In the Northeast, plant cannas as annuals, or lift rhizomes and store, replanting in the spring after risk of frost is past.

Dicentra eximia
FRINGED BLEEDING HEART
NATIVE HABITAT Northeastern U.S. forests
GROWTH TYPE Perennial herb, forming nonspreading clumps
HARDINESS ZONES 4 to 8
FLOWER COLOR Pink
HEIGHT 1 foot
BLOOMING PERIOD May to June; cut back in July for second blooming period in August.
HOW TO GROW Plant in rich, moist, porous soil; avoid letting water stand over roots; vegetation dies back in winter, so mark loca-

tion of plants to avoid disturbance during the dormant period.

CULTIVARS AND RELATED SPECIES 'Bacchanal' is a rhizomatous perennial with fine, gray-green leaves and 1-inch-long crimson flowers in mid- and late spring; grows 1 foot high with a spread of 2 feet. 'Luxuriant' is a hybrid between *D. eximia* and *D. peregrina* with crimson flowers capable of thriving in full sun.

Fuchsia species
FUCHSIAS

NATIVE HABITAT Mountainous regions of Central and South America; New Zealand

GROWTH TYPE Shrub or prostrate habit suitable for hanging baskets

HARDINESS ZONES 6 to 10, depending on species; typically grown as annual in the North.

FLOWER COLOR Almost any combination of white, pink, red, magenta, and purple; select varieties with simple red flowers to best attract hummingbirds.

HEIGHT 1 to 10 feet, depending on species

BLOOMING PERIOD

HOW TO GROW Fuchsias prefer cool, low-humidity conditions; avoid windy locations. Regular misting helps. Feed with a high-potassium fertilizer in summer to encourage continued flowering.

Fuchsia triphylla

CULTIVARS AND RELATED SPECIES *F. magellanica* produces small red flowers throughout the summer; in Zones 6 to 9, it can grow into a 10-foot-tall shrub with a spread of 6 to 10 feet. *F. triphylla* 'Mary' has many 1-inch, tubular crimson flowers born on upright woody stems.

Heuchera sanguinea
CORAL BELLS

NATIVE HABITAT Mexico and Arizona

GROWTH TYPE Clump-forming perennial noted for its rounded leaves

HARDINESS ZONES 3 to 8

FLOWER COLOR Pink to red

Heuchera sanguinea

flower clusters hang like tiny bells, rising about 1 to 2 feet above the ground on wiry stems.

HEIGHT The foliage is only a few inches tall but may spread to 2 feet.

BLOOMING PERIOD Spring to summer

HOW TO GROW Plant in sun or partial shade in rich soil with ample water; divide plants in early spring, removing dead growth.

CULTIVARS AND RELATED SPECIES *H.* × *brizoides* 'Firefly' features clusters of vermilion flowers borne on stems to 30 inches tall. *H. sanguinea* 'Firesprite' bears panicles of bright rose-red flowers on stiff, 20-inch stems. *H. sanguinea* 'Frosty' has silver-variegated leaves and bright red flowers on 20-inch stems.

Impatiens capensis
JEWELWEED

NATIVE HABITAT Forest understory and woodland edges in damp soils of eastern U.S.

GROWTH TYPE Herbaceous wildflower

HARDINESS ZONES Annual

FLOWER COLOR Orange

HEIGHT 1 to 3 feet

BLOOMING PERIOD Summer to fall

HOW TO GROW Collect seeds in early fall and scatter onto bare garden soil.

CULTIVARS AND RELATED SPECIES *I. pallida*, yellow jewelweed, grows 2 to 4 feet tall and occurs in more shaded habitats than *I. capensis*. Cultivated impatiens such as *I. balsamina* and New Guinea hybrid impatiens have less nectar than *I. capensis* and *I. pallida* and are therefore less useful for hummingbirds, even though bright colors may prove initially attractive.

Ipomoea coccinea
RED MORNING GLORY

NATIVE HABITAT Eastern North America

GROWTH TYPE Vine

HARDINESS ZONES Annual

FLOWER COLOR Clusters of 3 to 8 scarlet flowers with yellow throats

HEIGHT 6 to 12 feet
BLOOMING PERIOD Summer
HOW TO GROW Soak seeds for 24 hours and plant in well-drained soil in full sun.

Lobelia cardinalis
CARDINAL FLOWER

NATIVE HABITAT Eastern and southwestern U.S.
GROWTH TYPE Perennial herb
HARDINESS ZONES 3 to 9
FLOWER COLOR Many scarlet flowers arise from 12- to 18-inch flower stalks; white-, pink-, and violet-flowered varieties also occur, but these are less attractive to hummingbirds.
HEIGHT 2 to 3 feet
BLOOMING PERIOD Early to late summer
HOW TO GROW Purchase container-grown plants or grow from seed in damp soil in full sun.
CULTIVARS AND RELATED SPECIES *L. siphilitica*, great blue lobelia, is a clump-forming perennial with erect, leafy stems with tubular, two-lipped flowers.

Monarda didyma
BEE BALM, BERGAMOT, OSWEGO TEA

NATIVE HABITAT Eastern North America
GROWTH TYPE Clump-forming herbaceous perennial that can

Impatiens capensis

spread vigorously into adjacent areas
HARDINESS ZONES 4 to 9
FLOWER COLOR Scarlet, pink, or lavender flowers about 1 inch long appearing in one or two whorls at the ends of stems that arise above the leaves
HEIGHT 3 feet with a spread to 2 feet or more
BLOOMING PERIOD Early to late summer
HOW TO GROW Full or partial sun in well-drained soils; cut back after flowering.
CULTIVARS AND RELATED SPECIES *M. fistulosa*, wild bee balm, is a bushy, clump-forming perennial of

Monarda didyma

eastern North American meadows with purple or pale pink flowers in late summer and early fall; 4 feet high with a spread of 18 inches; Zones 3 to 9.

Osmunda cinnamomea
CINNAMON FERN

NATIVE HABITAT Most woodlands and forest edges of eastern North America

GROWTH TYPE Perennial; the cinnamon fuzz on the base of the fronds is a favorite hummingbird nest-lining material.

HARDINESS ZONES 4 to 8

FRUITING STRUCTURE Each fertile frond is topped by a mass of cinnamon-brown sporangia in spring.

HEIGHT 36 inches tall with a spread of 24 inches

HOW TO GROW Plant in moist fertile, acidic, humus-rich soil. Grows best in partial shade or dappled light.

Phaseolus coccineus
SCARLET RUNNER BEAN

NATIVE HABITAT Widely distributed

GROWTH TYPE Climbing or bush

HARDINESS ZONES Annual

FLOWER COLOR Scarlet

HEIGHT Climbing varieties reach 8 to 12 feet; bush varieties are self-supporting and grow to only 1 to 2 feet.

BLOOMING PERIOD Midsummer to early fall

HOW TO GROW Plant seeds in full sun long after risk of last frost. Support vines on a trellis or fence. Bush varieties can be grown in containers. Water frequently.

Polygonatum biflorum
SOLOMON'S SEAL

NATIVE HABITAT Forests of eastern North America

GROWTH TYPE Perennial herb

HARDINESS ZONES 3 to 9

FLOWER COLOR White, bell-shaped flowers that dangle from alternate leaf axils

HEIGHT 1 to 3 feet

Polygonatum biflorum

BLOOMING PERIOD Late spring to midsummer

HOW TO GROW Plant in a cool, shady location in fertile, well-drained soil; new growth occurs as rhizomes spread to adjacent habitat. Ideal for the north side of a building or another shady location.

Salvia splendens
SCARLET SAGE

NATIVE HABITAT Tropical South America

GROWTH TYPE Tender perennial

HARDINESS ZONES Usually grown in North America as annual.

FLOWER COLOR Scarlet-red flowers borne in slender spikes; selected varieties are available in a range of colors, but hummingbirds show a preference for the species.

HEIGHT 1 to 3 feet

BLOOMING PERIOD Summer to autumn

HOW TO GROW Part sun to shade, rich soil with plenty of water

CULTIVARS AND RELATED SPECIES *S. elegans*, pineapple sage, is an annual herb, 2 to 3 feet tall with woolly, light green leaves that have a fruity taste, and red flower spikes in the fall. *S. coccinea* 'Lady in Red', tropical sage, is a 1-foot-tall herb with scarlet-red flowers; treated in North American gardens as an annual.

Silene virginica
FIRE PINK

NATIVE HABITAT Open woods and rocky slopes in central and eastern U.S.

GROWTH TYPE Herbaceous short-lived perennial

HARDINESS ZONES 4 to 8

FLOWER COLOR Scarlet

HEIGHT 1 to 2 feet

BLOOMING PERIOD Spring and early summer

HOW TO GROW Partial shade in average, well-drained soil

CULTIVARS AND RELATED SPECIES *S. regia*, royal catchfly, and *S. rotundifolia*, round-leafed catchfly, are similar to fire pink, differing in flower and leaf shape. All three species have brilliant red petals and compelling nectar supplies.

Tropaeolum majus
NASTURTIUM

NATIVE HABITAT Cool, mountainous areas of Central and South America

GROWTH TYPE Trailing ground-cover or climber

HARDINESS ZONES Usually grown as an annual.

FLOWER COLOR 1- to 2-inch-long, red, orange, and yellow funnel-shaped flowers have five petals.

HEIGHT 3 to 10 feet, with a spread of 5 to 15 feet

BLOOMING PERIOD Summer to fall

HOW TO GROW Plant seeds in spring or nursery-grown small plants in spring or summer in full or partial sun.

CULTIVARS AND RELATED SPECIES Many dwarf varieties are derived from *T. majus*.

Zinnia elegans
ZINNIA

NATIVE HABITAT Mexico

GROWTH TYPE Upright, bushy herb

HARDINESS ZONES Annual

FLOWER COLOR Many colors and forms

HEIGHT 24 to 30 inches

BLOOMING PERIOD Summer to late fall or first frost

HOW TO GROW Plant seeds or greenhouse-grown plants in well-drained soil in full sun after the risk of frost; sow seeds in succession for a longer display.

CULTIVARS AND RELATED SPECIES Bright red cultivars such as 'Dreamland Scarlet' are most attractive to hummingbirds. After bloom, leave the dried seed heads on zinnias, which are eaten by goldfinches.

NOTE: Members of the sunflower family such as zinnias and coneflowers (*Echinacea angustifolia, E. purpurea*) produce relatively little nectar but are highly attractive to insects, an essential component of the hummingbird diet.

More Hummingbird Plants for the Northeast and Midwest

TREES

Cercis canadensis EASTERN REDBUD   Understory tree with pink, early-spring flowers; Zones 4 to 9

Liriodendron tulipifera TULIP TREE   Canopy tree with large, tulip-like green flowers with orange centers; Zones 5 to 9

SHRUBS

Cephalanthus occidentalis BUTTONBUSH   Shrub that thrives in damp soils; flowers in spring; Zones 4 to 8

Chaenomeles japonica FLOWERING QUINCE   Shrub with pink or orange flowers in spring; Zones 5 to 9

Lonicera canadensis FLY HONEYSUCKLE   5-foot-tall, native deciduous shrub with yellow, paired flowers; Zones 4 to 7

VINES

Campsis radicans TRUMPET CREEPER   Vine with orange or red tubular flowers; Zones 5 to 9

Lonicera sempervirens CORAL HONEYSUCKLE   Climbing vine or groundcover with coral-red tubular flowers; Zones 4 to 9

PERENNIALS AND ANNUALS

Castilleja coccinea INDIAN PAINTBRUSH   Annual or biennial; full sun with bright orange-red bracts; Zones 5 to 7

Chelone glabra TURTLEHEAD   Herbaceous perennial of damp soils with white to pale pink flowers; Zones 4 to 9

Delphinium nudicaule DELPHINIUM (LARKSPUR)   Perennial (Zones 6 to 9) and *D. grandiflorum*—annual; many cultivars

Hosta species HOSTA (PLANTAIN LILY)   Primarily foliage plant; shade tolerant with white or blue tubular flowers; Zones 3 to 8

Kniphofia uvaria RED HOT POKER   4-foot-tall native of South Africa; orange-yellow wands of tubular flowers; Zones 5 to 9

Penstemon digitalis FOXGLOVE BEARDTONGUE   White-flowered perennial tolerant of high heat and humidity; Zones 2 to 8. *P. hirsutus* has pale violet flowers; Zones 3 to 9.

Hummingbird Plants for the Southeast

by Jesse Grantham

Anisacanthus wrightii
TEXAS FIRECRACKER

NATIVE HABITAT Texas and adjacent Mexico

GROWTH TYPE Clumping herbaceous shrub

HARDINESS ZONES 7 to 10

FLOWER COLOR Long tubular flowers ranging from light orange to dark orange-red

HEIGHT 3 feet tall and 2 feet wide; in warmer areas with no frost, it can reach 6 feet.

BLOOMING PERIOD Late spring to mid-autumn, or until frost

HOW TO GROW Drought tolerant; thrives in full to partial sun in most soils; it readily self-seeds and can form colonies if allowed to spread. Prune in winter for compact shape and more blooms.

Left: *Salvia guaranitica* (see page 68)

CULTIVARS AND RELATED SPECIES
Thurber's desert honeysuckle, *A. thurberi*, a drought-tolerant, deciduous shrub, has orange to scarlet tubular flowers and is native to the Sonoran and Chihuahuan deserts of southern Arizona and New Mexico and northern Mexico; Zones 8 to 11.

Asclepias curassavica
SCARLET MILKWEED, BLOODFLOWER

NATIVE HABITAT South America

GROWTH TYPE Upright, evergreen subshrub

HARDINESS ZONES 8 to 11; treated as annual in cooler regions

FLOWER COLOR Orange and red flowers, borne in clusters at the tip of stems

HEIGHT 3 to 4 feet

BLOOMING PERIOD Spring to autumn

Cuphea micropetala

HOW TO GROW Thrives in full sun in moist soils; not as drought tolerant as other milkweeds.
CULTIVARS AND RELATED SPECIES *A. tuberosa*, a drought-tolerant, herbaceous annual, bears clusters of bright orange flowers and is native to prairies of the central and eastern U.S.

Bignonia capreolata
CROSS-VINE
NATIVE HABITAT Throughout the Southeast and as far north as Pennsylvania
GROWTH TYPE Climbing, clinging vine not unlike trumpet creeper
HARDINESS ZONES 7 to 9

FLOWER COLOR A broad, trumpet-shaped, red flower to 2 inches, with yellow tips. Some forms are entirely red.
HEIGHT Depends on support structure. Can cling to cement, masonry, or brick walls and grow to 20 feet.
BLOOMING PERIOD Flowers most profusely in early spring with occasional blooms throughout the summer
HOW TO GROW Grows best in full sun but tolerates partial shade of open woodland. In garden situation plant in deep, rich soil on a trellis, arbor, or side of brick or stone wall for best effect.

Campsis radicans
TRUMPET CREEPER
NATIVE HABITAT Throughout the southeastern U.S. to southern New England
GROWTH TYPE Climbing, clinging vine. Can grow up smooth surfaces using aerial roots.
HARDINESS ZONES 5 to 9
FLOWER COLOR Orange to orange-yellow flowers 2 to 4 inches long
HEIGHT Depends on support structure. Can scale telephone poles, tall trees, or buildings.
BLOOMING PERIOD Sporadically in spring; heavily in late summer through fall

HOW TO GROW In deep, rich topsoil in full sun on fences, trellis, or arbors. Prune throughout the summer to keep in check.

Cordia boissieri
TEXAS OLIVE

NATIVE HABITAT Coastal areas to dry semidesert regions of Texas and Mexico

GROWTH TYPE An evergreen, this medium-sized tree is evenly proportioned, with a rounded form.

HARDINESS ZONES 9 to 11; sensitive to subfreezing temperatures for any length of time. Light frost will kill leaves, but plant will leaf out in spring.

FLOWER COLOR Abundant beautiful white azalea-like flowers with yellow throats; favored by hummingbirds during spring migration

HEIGHT Tall specimens may reach 8 to 10 feet.

BLOOMING PERIOD During spring months and sometimes again in fall

HOW TO GROW This tree grows in full sun or open shade in hot humid or dry regions. Can be grown in many different soil types, from rich sandy loam to sand or caliche (hardpan); very drought tolerant; requires regular watering during first year after planting.

Erythrina herbacea (see page 64)

Cuphea micropetala
MEXICAN CIGAR

NATIVE HABITAT Mexico to Central America

GROWTH TYPE Small mounded shrub to about 3 feet

HARDINESS ZONES 8 to 9; not terribly frost tolerant but can be grown as an annual in more temperate areas.

FLOWER COLOR Bright red, tubular flowers with yellow tips, about 1 inch long

HEIGHT 1 to 3 feet

BLOOMING PERIOD Summer through fall

SOUTHEAST

Ipomoea quamoclit

HOW TO GROW Grows well along borders or as a foundation plant in full sun to partial light shade.

CULTIVARS AND RELATED SPECIES *C. hyssopifolia,* an evergreen sub-shrub from Mexico and Guatemala, is also popular with hummingbirds.

Erythrina herbacea
CORAL BEAN

NATIVE HABITAT Southeastern U.S. west to Texas and south to Mexico in open fields, woodland, and oak copses (mottes)

GROWTH TYPE Upright herbaceous perennial to small, twiggy shrub

HARDINESS ZONES 9 to 10

FLOWER COLOR Dull pink to scarlet-red, long, tapered, tubular flowers

HEIGHT 2 feet

BLOOMING PERIOD Early spring; in more temperate areas flowers appear before foliage

HOW TO GROW Can grow in sand, caliche (hardpan), or rich woodland soil; generally drought tolerant. Prefers full sun to very light shade; fairly tolerant of light freezes but will die back to the ground. Difficult to move well-established plants.

CULTIVARS AND RELATED SPECIES *E. crista-galli*, native to eastern South America, has treelike growth habit and large red flowers. Can take short freezes. Both species visited by orioles in spring.

Hamelia patens
FIREBUSH

NATIVE HABITAT Southern Florida to Central and South America

GROWTH TYPE Robust, full, round-topped shrub with gray-green leaves

HARDINESS ZONE 9 to 10; grown as annual in cooler regions

FLOWER COLOR Leaf stalks as well as flowers are red.

HEIGHT 3 to 10 feet in good growing conditions

BLOOMING PERIOD Summer throughout fall

HOW TO GROW A great hummingbird plant, this small shrub does best in full sun but tolerates some light shade. Requires good moisture and well-drained soil. Summer growth is rapid and full. In the Deep South established plants can withstand brief temperatures below freezing, although the plant will die back to the ground.

Ipomoea quamoclit
CYPRESS VINE

NATIVE HABITAT Throughout the Southeast

GROWTH TYPE Twining vine

HARDINESS ZONES Annual

FLOWER COLOR A scarlet-red, trumpet-shaped flower to 1 inch

HEIGHT Depending on support structure, can climb to 20 feet

BLOOMING PERIOD Throughout the summer

HOW TO GROW Prefers rich, well-drained soil. Seedlings appear in spring under last year's plant. Purchase nursery-started plants in spring for quicker growth.

Justicia brandegeana
SHRIMP PLANT

NATIVE HABITAT Native to Mexico but naturalized in some places on the Texas Coastal Plain

Justicia brandegeana

GROWTH TYPE Herbaceous; this sprawling to leggy plant will grow up among branches of shrubs and small trees.

HARDINESS ZONES 8 to 9 (Established plants can survive light frost in more temperate climates.)

FLOWER COLOR White tubular flowers speckled with pink emerge from pink to red bracts.

HEIGHT 1 to 4 or 5 feet when growing among shrubs

BLOOMING PERIOD Spring to fall

HOW TO GROW Full sun to light shade; does well as container plant and can be kept indoors in winter. Survives frost when planted as a foundation plant on south-facing wall in more temperate climates.

SOUTHEAST

Lonicera sempervirens

CULTIVARS AND RELATED SPECIES
There are many species of *Justicia,*
all favored by hummingbirds.
J. spicigera, native to dry areas of
the Southwest and Mexico, grows
best in the Southeast as a foundation plant on south-facing walls;
Zones 9 to 10.

Lonicera sempervirens
CORAL HONEYSUCKLE
NATIVE HABITAT Edges of deciduous woodlands, field hedgerows,
open woodlands from Mexico as
far north as lower New England
states
GROWTH TYPE Nonaggressive,
twining vine

HARDINESS ZONES 5 to 9; can take
prolonged freezes
FLOWER COLOR Loose clusters of
red to orange-red or even red-
dish-yellow, 2-inch-long,
trumpet-shaped flowers with
orange tips
HEIGHT Depends on support
structure. Will grow up to 20 feet
on fences, trellises, and small
trees.
BLOOMING PERIOD Throughout
the growing season, with one or
two periods of heavy bloom in
spring or fall
HOW TO GROW Does best in fertile garden soil in full sun with
adequate water. Plants in shade
have fewer blooms and generate
more vegetative growth.

Malvaviscus arboreus var.
drummondii
SLEEPY MALLOW,
SULTAN'S TURBAN
NATIVE HABITAT Open sunny
glades, roadsides, or understory of
oak copses with partial sun. Common along Gulf Coastal Plain.
GROWTH TYPE Rather upright,
leggy perennial in partial shade;
sturdy upright perennial in full sun
HARDINESS ZONES 7 to 9
FLOWER COLOR Bright scarlet-
red, upright, closed flowers at the
top of branches or leaf clusters
HEIGHT 1 to 8 feet

BLOOMING PERIOD Throughout the growing season and until the onset of cool weather
HOW TO GROW Sleepy mallow grows in many different soil types, from sand or caliche (hardpan) to rich, deep loamy soils. It can tolerate drought conditions and does well in perennial borders and foundation plantings in full sun to partial shade. It is deciduous in colder zones from Florida to Texas and hardy north to the Tennessee-Mississippi border.

Rhododendron minus
PIEDMONT RHODODENDRON
NATIVE HABITAT Deciduous woodlands and mountains of Southeast
GROWTH TYPE Small spreading shrub
HARDINESS ZONES 6 to 8
FLOWER COLOR Clusters of deep red to pink flowers
HEIGHT 3 to 6 feet
BLOOMING PERIOD Spring
HOW TO GROW Will do best planted in rich soil in wooded understory on slopes. A wonderful plant for a woodland garden but can be tricky to grow because of variations in soil pH. Mulch with pine needles or compost.
CULTIVARS AND RELATED SPECIES Many species of *Rhododendron* are available; to attract hummingbirds and moths, use only native species.

Russelia equisetiformis
FIRECRACKER PLANT
NATIVE HABITAT Mexico and Central America
GROWTH TYPE Loose upright to weeping plant with bright green, pencil-sized stems
HARDINESS ZONE 9 to 10
FLOWER COLOR Small, bright red, tubular flowers, 1 inch long
HEIGHT 1 to 3 feet tall; long stems can be tied to stakes for upright growth.
BLOOMING PERIOD Throughout summer and fall in hot climates
HOW TO GROW Firecracker plant does well in sandy to rich loam soils. and is fairly drought tolerant. it spreads from roots, sending up shoots around its base. Even established plants have difficulty surviving below freezing temperatures for any length of time, but the plant is readily available for replanting where killing frost occurs.

Salvia coccinea
TROPICAL SAGE
NATIVE HABITAT Throughout the tropics; in recent years has spread to tropical North America.
GROWTH TYPE Rather loose, upright annual to perennial in milder climates
HARDINESS ZONES 9 to 10

SOUTHEAST

Salvia coccinea

FLOWER COLOR Many varieties from deep red to pink and white
HEIGHT To 3 feet
BLOOMING PERIOD Throughout the growing season
HOW TO GROW In milder regions of the Southeast, this plant can be a perennial. Cooler temperatures will reduce it to a basal rosette in winter. Heavy frost or a freeze will kill the plant, but seeds survive the winter and germinate in spring. Start with 6- to 8-inch nursery-started plants in spring in loamy garden soil. Seedlings will appear where last year's plants bloomed. Requires occasional watering during dry periods in summer.

Salvia guaranitica
ANISE SAGE
NATIVE HABITAT Widespread in South America
GROWTH TYPE Sturdy upright perennial
HARDINESS ZONES 8 to 9
FLOWER COLOR Deep, rich blue; flowers tubular and lipped at ends (see photo, page 60)
HEIGHT 1 to 5 feet
BLOOMING PERIOD Summer to fall
HOW TO GROW Prefers generally well-drained garden soil in full sun to partial shade. Will need water during prolonged summer dry periods. In colder areas throughout the Southeast can be grown as an annual.

Salvia leucantha
MEXICAN BUSH SAGE
NATIVE HABITAT Higher elevations in central and eastern Mexico
GROWTH TYPE Multistemmed perennial throughout its cultivated range in the U.S.
HARDINESS ZONES 7 to 9
FLOWER COLOR Curved, tubular flowers are white and emerge from a purple calyx.
HEIGHT Can grow up to 4 feet in a season and 3 to 5 feet in diameter.
BLOOMING PERIOD Generally from late summer to frost, like most salvias.

Salvia leucantha

SOUTHEAST

HOW TO GROW Can grow in sandy to rich, well-drained soil; does best in full sun and is drought tolerant. Prune dead stalks to ground after frost. Can withstand freezing temperatures for short periods, but tops will die back to the ground. In cooler areas of the Southeast, works best as a foundation planting.

Salvia lyrata
LYRE-LEAFED SAGE

NATIVE HABITAT Meadows of the Southeast
GROWTH TYPE Single stalk arising from a rosette of basal leaves
HARDINESS ZONES 7 to 8

FLOWER COLOR Pale blue to white
HEIGHT 1 to 2 feet
BLOOMING PERIOD For a month in early spring
HOW TO GROW Naturalizes in open lawns and meadows. Start from seed, then mow lawns or meadows after flowering is over. This encourages dense stands.

Salvia regla
MOUNTAIN SAGE

NATIVE HABITAT From the Chisos Mountains of Texas south to Mexico
GROWTH TYPE In warmer climates it can be a rather robust, multistemmed small shrub.

Tecomaria capensis

HARDINESS ZONES 8 to 9; can withstand temperatures down to 20 °F. for short periods.

FLOWER COLOR Deep rosy red

HEIGHT 6 feet tall and to 5 feet wide in protected and warm locations

BLOOMING PERIOD Like many salvias, this is a fall-blooming plant. Will bloom until there is a frost or days grow short.

HOW TO GROW In cooler climates does best on east- or south-facing walls with light shade. In warmer climates does well in any garden setting with partial shade. Prefers good soil and drainage.

Tecomaria capensis
CAPE HONEYSUCKLE

NATIVE HABITAT South Africa

GROWTH TYPE Long-stemmed, sprawling shrub that can be trained to a trellis or fence; can stand on its own with frequent pruning.

HARDINESS ZONES 8 to 9

FLOWER COLOR Vivid orange to yellow tubular flowers; cultivars may be salmon, apricot, scarlet, or gold.

HEIGHT Up to 20 feet when trained to climb

BLOOMING PERIOD Late summer through winter; in milder climates it will flower sporadically through-out the winter into spring.

HOW TO GROW Grows in poor, sandy to rich garden soils and tol-erates hot, windy coastal conditions. Plant along fence or wall as a foundation planting or standing alone. Established plants can withstand brief cold snaps of below-freezing temperatures. Spreads by underground roots and can be aggressive.

CULTIVARS AND RELATED SPECIES 'Aurea' and 'Lutea' produce golden to bright yellow flowers; 'Apricot' is orange; 'Coccinea' is scarlet; 'Salmonea' has pale pink to orange blooms.

More Hummingbird Plants for the Southeast

TREES
Aesculus pavia RED BUCKEYE   Understory large shrub to small tree of deep deciduous forests with striking racemes of bright red, tubular flowers in early spring before other trees are in full leaf; Zones 5 to 8

SHRUBS
Odontonema tubaeforme FIRE SPIKE   Tropical evergreen that grows in full sun to partial shade; crimson-red flowers borne on terminal spikes until hard frost; Zones 8 to 9

Rhododendron viscosum SWAMP AZALEA   Medium-sized shrub of moist woodland edges; pale red flowers with white edging in early spring; Zones 7 to 8

VINES
Pseudogynoxys chenopodioides MEXICAN FLAME VINE   8- to 10-foot vine with big clusters of 1-inch, orange-red flowers; year-round bloom where winters are mild—Zones 9 to 10

PERENNIALS AND ANNUALS
Heuchera americana CORAL BELLS   Perennial grown mainly for its foliage, with 3-foot spikes covered with small greenish-white flowers in early spring; Zones 4 to 8

Lobelia cardinalis CARDINAL FLOWER   Native perennial to 18 inches tall with scarlet flowers that bloom from early to late summer; damp soil and full sun; Zones 3 to 9

Mertensia virginica VIRGINIA BLUEBELLS   Native to the eastern U.S., usually found along streams or in alluvial plains; loose clusters of drooping blue flowers on 1- to 2-foot stems in early spring; foliage dieback in summer; Zones 3 to 7

Monarda fistulosa WILD BEE BALM   Bushy, clump-forming perennial native to the eastern U.S., usually in meadows, with purple or pale pink flowers; 4 feet tall with a spread of 18 inches; Zones 3 to 9

Top: *Bouvardia ternifolia*
Bottom: *Calliandra eriophylla*

Hummingbird Plants for the Western Mountains and Deserts

by Lynn Hassler Kaufman

Bouvardia ternifolia
SMOOTH BOUVARDIA

NATIVE HABITAT Dry shady slopes and canyons of southern New Mexico and Arizona; 3,000 to 9,000 feet

GROWTH TYPE Bouvardia belongs to a largely tropical family. This handsome shrub with evergreen foliage has narrow, trumpetlike flowers that flare into four lobes.

HARDINESS ZONES 6 to 8

FLOWER COLOR Clusters of bright red-orange (sometimes pink or white) honeysuckle-type flowers

HEIGHT 2 to 3 feet

BLOOMING PERIOD May to October

HOW TO GROW Prefers partial shade and supplemental water.

CULTIVARS AND RELATED SPECIES Many cultivars are available, with flower colors ranging from pale pink to red.

Calliandra californica
BAJA FAIRY DUSTER

NATIVE HABITAT Gravelly flats, hillsides, and washes in the central desert of Baja California, Mexico

GROWTH TYPE This shrub has flowers like fluffy balls or brushes. It's rich in nectar and insect life and is extremely popular with hummingbirds.

HARDINESS ZONES 9 to 10

FLOWER COLOR Spectacular bright red powder-puff blooms

HEIGHT 4 to 5 feet

BLOOMING PERIOD Nearly year-round in warmer desert areas

HOW TO GROW Plant in full sun for optimal blooming; tolerates light shade. Not picky about soil type. Natural growth form is attractive and needs no shaping.
CULTIVARS AND RELATED SPECIES Fairy duster (*C. eriophylla*) is native to southwestern U.S. and Mexico. Generally found at 1,000 to 5,000 feet in sandy washes and on dry gravelly slopes and mesas. Flowers (primarily February to May) range from nearly white to deep pink. Hardy to 10°F.; drought tolerant. Foliage is evergreen to semievergreen, depending on temperatures and availability of moisture.

Castilleja integra
INDIAN PAINTBRUSH
NATIVE HABITAT Dryish rocky slopes among oaks and pines in Colorado, western Texas, New Mexico, Arizona, and northern Mexico; 4,500 to 10,000 feet
GROWTH TYPE Herbaceous perennial; there are more than 200 species of paintbrush in the West, and they are important hummingbird plants.
HARDINESS ZONES 5 to 8
FLOWER COLOR The true petals are inconspicuous and usually green; the large splashes of color (in this species, vermilion) are the brightly colored leafy bracts.

HEIGHT To 1 foot
BLOOMING PERIOD March to September
HOW TO GROW Most paintbrushes are partial root parasites, and seeds need to be planted with seeds of another plant (such as blue grama grass, for this species). Long-lived when grown with a suitable host. Likes well-drained soil.
CULTIVARS AND RELATED SPECIES Desert paintbrush (*Castilleja chromosa*), with orange bracts, is native to open sagebrush flats, at 5,000 to 8,000 feet, from eastern Oregon to Wyoming and south to New Mexico and Southern California.

Cirsium arizonicum
ARIZONA THISTLE
NATIVE HABITAT Rocky slopes and roadsides in Utah and Arizona; 3,000 to 7,000 feet
GROWTH TYPE Biennial
HARDINESS ZONES 6 to 8
FLOWER COLOR Red
HEIGHT 2 feet
BLOOMING PERIOD May to October
HOW TO GROW Although thistles are considered weeds in many parts of the country, this species does not seem to reseed readily. Grow in full sun in well-drained

Right: *Castilleja chromosa*

soil. Plant away from walkways since the foliage is spiny and prickly. Nursery plants may be difficult to find, but seeds are available.

CULTIVARS AND RELATED SPECIES New Mexico thistle (*C. neomexicanum*) grows at altitudes from 1,000 to 6,500 feet in the Southwest; it has lavender blooms from March to September.

Delphinium occidentale
WESTERN LARKSPUR

NATIVE HABITAT Moist mountain meadows in the Rocky Mountains and northern Southwest
GROWTH TYPE Herbaceous perennial
HARDINESS ZONES 4 to 5
FLOWER COLOR Tall spires of blue-purple blooms
HEIGHT 3 to 6 feet
BLOOMING PERIOD June to August
HOW TO GROW Full sun or partial shade. Seeds are available from native-plant catalogs.

Erythrina flabelliformis
SOUTHWEST CORAL BEAN

NATIVE HABITAT Rocky canyons and hillsides in southeastern Arizona, southwestern New Mexico, and north Mexico, including Baja; 3,000 to 5,500 feet
GROWTH TYPE Shrub; when in flower or fruit, this plant is striking.

At other times it has leafless brown stems.
HARDINESS ZONES 8 to 10
FLOWER COLOR Clusters of bright red, tubular flowers
HEIGHT 3 to 6 feet; can reach tree size in warmer areas of Mexico
BLOOMING PERIOD Spring; sometimes again after summer rains
HOW TO GROW Plant in warm location in well-drained soil. Full sun. Prune frost-damaged wood after new foliage appears. The bright red seeds are poisonous.

Fouquieria splendens
OCOTILLO

NATIVE HABITAT Arizona, California, and Texas deserts; rocky hillsides below 5,000 feet
GROWTH TYPE Thorny shrub with long, unbranched stems and flame-colored spring blooms—a distinctive accent plant. The stems are popular perches for hummingbirds.
HARDINESS ZONES 7 to 8
FLOWER COLOR Dense clusters of bright red, tubular blossoms appear at branch tips.
HEIGHT To 15 feet
BLOOMING PERIOD April to June, but may bloom at other seasons
HOW TO GROW Plant in full sun in well-drained soil. Susceptible to overwatering. Drops leaves when conditions are dry and leafs out in response to moisture, up to several

times a year. If pruning is necessary, cut branches away at the base. Individual canelike stems root readily and make "living fences" that develop roots, leaves, and sometimes flowers.

Hesperaloe parviflora
RED YUCCA

NATIVE HABITAT Prairies, rocky slopes, mesquite groves in central and southwestern Texas and northern Mexico

GROWTH TYPE Evergreen perennial; this member of the agave family has an attractive form and texture and makes a nice accent plant.

Hesperaloe parviflora

HARDINESS ZONES 7 to 10

FLOWER COLOR Coral or salmon bell-shaped flowers in clusters; a yellow-flowering variety is also available

HEIGHT Flower stalks reach 5 feet

BLOOMING PERIOD Spring to fall

HOW TO GROW Full sun or partial shade in well-drained soil; drought tolerant. Prune back flower stalks after blooming.

Heuchera versicolor
CORAL BELLS

NATIVE HABITAT Moist, shaded rocky areas in coniferous forests in southwestern U.S. and northern Mexico; 6,500 to 12,000 feet

GROWTH TYPE Herbaceous perennial; dainty flower stalks arise from clumps of evergreen leaves.

HARDINESS ZONES 5 to 8

FLOWER COLOR Mainly pink

HEIGHT 6- to 10-inch stalks

BLOOMING PERIOD May to October

HOW TO GROW Plant in shade or partial shade and provide ample water. Clumps may need to be divided after several years.

CULTIVARS AND RELATED SPECIES *H. sanguinea*, with red flowers, is native to southeastern Arizona and Mexico at elevations of 4,000 to 8,500 feet. Many varieties of coral bells are available.

Ipomopsis aggregata
SCARLET GILIA,
SKYROCKET

NATIVE HABITAT Montana to British Columbia, south to New Mexico, Arizona, and California, mostly in open coniferous forests; 5,000 to 8,500 feet

GROWTH TYPE Biennial

HARDINESS ZONES 5 to 8

FLOWER COLOR Normally bright red but also pink or white; in some areas this showy wildflower changes color in response to changes in pollinators. Early in the season, red flowers are most common, coinciding with the abundance of hummingbirds in mountainous regions. By late August, new flowering plants produce mainly light pink and white flowers, as most hummingbirds depart and sphinx moths take over as the main pollinators.

HEIGHT 2 feet

BLOOMING PERIOD May to September

HOW TO GROW Likes well-drained soil and full sun; individual plants are on the thin side, so the plant looks best in mass plantings.

Justicia californica
CHUPAROSA

NATIVE HABITAT Rocky slopes and along washes in desert areas of southern Arizona, southeastern California into Mexico; 1,000 to 4,000 feet

GROWTH TYPE Shrub;

HARDINESS ZONES 8 to 10

FLOWER COLOR Bright red; a yellow-flowering variety is available in the landscape trade. The slender floral tubes contain abundant nectar irrestistible to hummers. *Chuparosa* means "hummingbird" in Spanish.

HEIGHT 3 feet tall and 4 feet wide; 6 feet under ideal conditions

BLOOMING PERIOD Heaviest in spring but also summer, fall, and winter if not killed back by frost

HOW TO GROW Plant in full sun. Very drought tolerant once established. Can be grown on 10 inches or less of annual rainfall, but periodic watering will improve appearance.

CULTIVARS AND RELATED SPECIES Red justicia (*J. candicans*) sports lush green leaves and bright red-orange flowers February to May. Native to canyons and washes in southern Arizona and northern Mexico; 1,500 to 3,500 feet.

Lycium andersonii
WOLFBERRY

NATIVE HABITAT Desert washes and rocky slopes to 6,000 feet in southern Utah and Nevada, Arizona, southwestern New Mexico, and northwestern Mexico

Nicotiana glauca

GROWTH TYPE Shrub; in addition to the short tubular flowers that attract hummingbirds, this dense, spiny shrub also produces berries that are relished by many other kinds of birds.
HARDINESS ZONES 7 to 10
FLOWER COLOR Pale lavender
HEIGHT 6 feet
BLOOMING PERIOD February to May
HOW TO GROW Plants of many species of *Lycium* are now available in one-gallon containers. Plant in full sun or light shade in well-drained soil. Best left unpruned. Becomes leafless in response to drought and cold.

CULTIVARS AND RELATED SPECIES Many species of wolfberry, including *L. berlandieri*, *L. exsertum*, and *L. fremontii*, look rather similar and have the same white to purplish flowers that are visited by hummingbirds.

Nicotiana glauca
TREE TOBACCO

NATIVE HABITAT Southern Bolivia to northern Argentina: naturalized extensively in many parts of the West and Southeast
GROWTH TYPE This shrubby, rather weedy-looking evergreen tree is often seen growing by roadsides. The abundant flowers are

Penstemon barbatus

very popular with hummingbirds, moths, and butterflies.

HARDINESS ZONES 7 to 10

FLOWER COLOR Yellow-green tubular flowers

HEIGHT Up to 20 feet

BLOOMING PERIOD Sporadically throughout the year in warm climates

HOW TO GROW Full sun to partial shade in moist, well-drained, deep soil. Short lived but fast growing. Prune frequently for compact growth. Tree tobacco reseeds readily and become weedy, so trim faded flowers to avoid seed production.

Penstemon barbatus
SCARLET BUGLER

NATIVE HABITAT Mountains in coniferous or oak woodlands of southern Colorado and Utah to Mexico; 4,000 to 10,000 feet

GROWTH TYPE Herbaceous perennial

HARDINESS ZONES 5 to 8

FLOWER COLOR Tubular red flowers in loose spikes; the lower lip of the flower in this species is bent back so hummingbirds can hover to sip the nectar. Bees and butterflies must perch to feed and have no foothold.

HEIGHT 1 to 3 feet

BLOOMING PERIOD June to October

HOW TO GROW Well-drained soil, sun to partial shade. May be short-lived in warm winter areas.

CULTIVARS AND RELATED SPECIES Firecracker penstemon (*P. eatonii*) grows on rocky slopes of the Southwest; 2,000 to 7,000 feet. Prefers well-drained soil in full sun to partial shade. Tubular scarlet flowers bloom March to June. Pineleaf penstemon (*P. pinifolius*) grows on outcroppings and steep slopes from 6,000 to 8,500 feet from southern Arizona and New Mexico into Mexico. Small scarlet flowers on 10- to 12-inch spikes attract White-eared Hummingbirds in Mexico.

Penstemon parryi
PARRY PENSTEMON

NATIVE HABITAT Washes, desert slopes, and canyons of southern Arizona and Sonora, Mexico; 1,500 to 5,000 feet

GROWTH TYPE Herbaceous, usually evergreen perennial; penstemons make up a very large genus of plants, and there are species available for nearly every climate.

HARDINESS ZONES 8 to 10

FLOWER COLOR Deep pink, tubular flowers

HEIGHT 2- to 3-foot flower spikes arise from basal rosette of foliage.

BLOOMING PERIOD February to April

HOW TO GROW Well-drained soil, full sun. Do not overwater. Spent flower spikes can be cut off after they have gone to seed. Reseeds freely.

CULTIVARS AND RELATED SPECIES Rock penstemon (*P. baccharifolius*) grows in limestone soils in west Texas at altitudes from 1,100 to 4,400 feet. Cherry-red flowers on short spikes bloom throughout the hot season in the low desert (June to September). Needs excellent drainage and prefers partial shade to full sun. Prune off old flower stalks to improve the plant's appearance.

Penstemon parryi

Penstemon superbus
SUPERB PENSTEMON

NATIVE HABITAT Rocky canyons and washes in New Mexico, southeastern Arizona, and Chihuahua, Mexico; 3,500 to 5,500 feet

GROWTH TYPE Herbaceous perennial

HARDINESS ZONES 7 to 10

FLOWER COLOR Dark coral

HEIGHT Stalks reach 3 to 4 feet

BLOOMING PERIOD April to May

HOW TO GROW In full sun; likes sandy or gravelly soils

CULTIVARS AND RELATED SPECIES See *P. barbatus* and *P. parryi*.

WESTERN MOUNTAINS & DESERTS

Top: *Salvia greggii*
Bottom: *Stachys coccinea*

Salvia greggii
RED SAGE, AUTUMN SAGE

NATIVE HABITAT Rocky canyons from 2,200 to 5,800 feet in the Chihuahuan Desert region

GROWTH TYPE Small, rounded evergreen shrub, good for xeriscape plantings and mixed borders. It may bloom lightly throughout the year in warmer areas, providing a reliable nectar source for hummingbirds.

HARDINESS ZONES 7 to 10

FLOWER COLOR Spikes of tubular flowers in shades of rose pink; many color variants are available, but those with reddish hues are particularly attractive to hummers.

HEIGHT 3 feet

BLOOMING PERIOD March to November

HOW TO GROW Partial shade to full sun. Needs good drainage. Prune back hard to keep plants from becoming too woody.

CULTIVARS AND RELATED SPECIES Mountain sage or cardinal sage (*S. regla*) is a fall bloomer in western Texas. Grows 3 to 5 feet tall (sometimes to 8 feet) and produces masses of brilliant vermilion flowers. Cedar sage (*S. roemeriana*) is a low-growing perennial about 1 foot tall and wide with scarlet flowers March to August. Prefers dappled shade. Native to western Texas and Mexico.

Tecoma stans (see page 84)

Silene laciniata
INDIAN PINK, MEXICAN CAMPION

NATIVE HABITAT Western Texas to California and Mexico, mostly in pine forests; 5,500 to 9,000 feet

GROWTH TYPE Perennial herb; at first glance the flower petals seem separate rather than fused into tubes. A closer look reveals that the lower part of each petal is confined within a tubular calyx, thus displaying the tubular shape that is so attractive to hummingbirds.

HARDINESS ZONES 5 to 7

FLOWER COLOR Red

HEIGHT To 3 feet

BLOOMING PERIOD July to October

HOW TO GROW Partial shade; likes to lean against other vegetation. May be difficult to find; try native-plant nurseries or catalogs.

Stachys coccinea
SCARLET OR TEXAS BETONY

NATIVE HABITAT Canyons and slopes in west Texas to southern Arizona and Mexico; 1,500 to 8,000 feet

GROWTH TYPE Herbaceous perennial; evergreen in warmer areas; flowers from spring to frost, with denser blooms when spent flower spikes removed.

HARDINESS ZONES 7 to 9

FLOWER COLOR Vermilion

WESTERN MOUNTAINS & DESERTS

HEIGHT 18 inches tall and 24 inches wide

BLOOMING PERIOD Spring through fall

HOW TO GROW Likes rich soil; requires additional water or light to medium shade to survive summer heat in high desert.

Tecoma stans
YELLOW BELLS

NATIVE HABITAT Rocky slopes, gravelly plains, and arroyos in southeastern Arizona, southern New Mexico, west Texas, south into Mexico, Central and South America; 2,000 to 5,000 feet

GROWTH TYPE Deciduous shrub; the lush foliage and showy blooms of this plant give it a tropical look.

HARDINESS ZONES 7 to 9

FLOWER COLOR Yellow trumpet-shaped flowers in large clusters

HEIGHT To 5 feet

BLOOMING PERIOD April to November

HOW TO GROW Full sun and well-drained soil. Recovers quickly after frost and can grow 4 feet in a season.

More Hummingbird Plants for the Western Mountains and Deserts

TREES

Chilopsis linearis DESERT WILLOW   Tree of dry washes with pink to lavender trumpet-shaped flowers in clusters, April to September; Zones 7 to 10

SHRUBS

Galvezia juncea GALVEZIA   Baja California native bearing scarlet tubular flowers on and off all year; to 6 feet; Zones 9 to 10

Salvia leucantha MEXICAN BUSH SAGE   Mexican native with long, slender, velvety-purple or deep rose spikes with small white flowers; full sun; drought tolerant; periodic pruning to prevent woodiness; Zones 9 to 10

Tecomaria capensis CAPE HONEYSUCKLE   Shrub or vine native to South Africa; showy orange flowers in fall and winter; Zones 9 to 10

VINES

Ipomoea coccinea RED MORNING GLORY   Long twining vine with reddish-orange tubular flowers from May to October; Zones 7 to 10

PERENNIALS AND ANNUALS

Agastache cana GIANT HYSSOP/WILD HYSSOP   2- to 3-foot-tall, rose-pink flower spikes from midsummer to fall; aromatic leaves; Zones 6 to 7

Epilobium canum subsp. *latifolia* (formerly *Zauschneria californica* subsp. *latifolia*) CALIFORNIA FUCHSIA/HUMMINGBIRD FUCHSIA   Perennial with bright red-orange, trumpet-shaped flowers in late summer and fall; Zones 7 to 10

Lobelia cardinalis CARDINAL FLOWER   Perennial with bright red, inch-long flowers from June to October; moist soils; Zones 5 to 8

Mimulus cardinalis CRIMSON MONKEYFLOWER   Perennial with funnel-shaped red flowers March to October; moist soils and shade; Zones 6 to 9

Russelia equisetiformis CORAL FOUNTAIN   Shrubby perennial native to Mexico with bright red tubular flowers from spring to fall; moist soils; Zones 9 to 10

Chilopsis linearis

WESTERN MOUNTAINS & DESERTS

Hummingbird Plants for the Pacific Coast

by Beth Huning

Aquilegia formosa
WESTERN COLUMBINE

NATIVE HABITAT Meadows and damp areas of western mountains, Pacific Northwest, and Alaska

GROWTH TYPE Short-lived perennial; erect stems to 18 inches from low-growing plant

HARDINESS ZONES 6 to 9

FLOWER COLOR Scarlet-red or orange backward-projecting petals with contrasting yellow sepals and protruding stamens. Flowers are erect or nodding.

HEIGHT 2 to 3 feet

BLOOMING PERIOD Spring to summer

HOW TO GROW Hardy; tolerates filtered shade, although will thrive in full sun, especially along coast or in mountains if planted in moist, rich soils. Will self-seed but plants can also be divided in spring.

CULTIVARS AND RELATED SPECIES
Native and hybridized columbine flowers range from $1^1/_2$ to 3 inches with a variety of color combinations, including white, yellow, blues, and purples in addition to the red-orange and yellow combinations of *A. formosa* and *A. canadensis*. Plants range from 2 to 4 feet tall. Other species include *A. brevistyla* (western mountains and Alaska) and *A. canadensis*, wild columbine (rocky slopes and alkaline soils in eastern North America).

Castilleja coccinea
INDIAN PAINTBRUSH

NATIVE HABITAT Dry slopes of the western U.S.

GROWTH TYPE Herbaceous perennial or biennial

HARDINESS ZONES 6 to 9

FLOWER COLOR Clustered spikes of scarlet bracts

HEIGHT 6 to 12 inches

BLOOMING PERIOD Spring to mid-autumn

HOW TO GROW Must be grown from seed near other plants whose roots it parasitizes, such as penstemons. Prefers wet, well-drained soils in full sun.

CULTIVARS AND RELATED SPECIES This is an important hummingbird plant in the western United States. Species range in habitat and distribution from dry slopes at low elevations to high mountains. The many species of paintbrush include *C. applegatei* subsp. *pinetorum* with scarlet, sometimes orange or yellow, bracts. Look for seeds at native plant nurseries.

Aquilegia formosa

Chilopsis linearis
DESERT WILLOW

NATIVE HABITAT Open areas and stream courses of deserts and the basin and ranges of the southwestern U.S.

GROWTH TYPE Shrub; sometimes becomes treelike

HARDINESS ZONES 7 to 9

FLOWER COLOR Purplish to pink, sometimes orange to yellow trumpet-shaped flowers

HEIGHT Up to 20 feet high and broad

BLOOMING PERIOD Late spring through late summer, depending upon elevation and exposure to sun.

HOW TO GROW Thrives in direct sun in dry, open areas. Drought tolerant; deciduous from late summer through midwinter.

CULTIVARS AND RELATED SPECIES Also known as desert catalpa, *Chilopsis* is not a true willow (*Salix* species), but its elliptical leaves resemble those of willows, hence its common name.

Delphinium cardinale
SCARLET LARKSPUR

NATIVE HABITAT California coastal mountains south of Monterey

GROWTH TYPE Herbaceous perennial, sometimes treated as annual; robust with tall stems from woody roots

PACIFIC COAST

HARDINESS ZONES 8 to 9
FLOWER COLOR Red with narrow yellow lobes
HEIGHT 3 to 6 feet
BLOOMING PERIOD Late spring, early summer
HOW TO GROW Grows in full or filtered sun in rich, alkaline soils. Fertilize regularly; no water necessary in late summer. Sow seed early for spring blooms.

Delphinium nudicaule
ORANGE LARKSPUR
NATIVE HABITAT Northern California and southwestern Oregon
GROWTH TYPE Herbaceous perennial, often treated as annual. Slender form, sparsely blooming flowers.
HARDINESS ZONES 7 to 9
FLOWER COLOR Red with long spurs
HEIGHT 1 to 3 feet
BLOOMING PERIOD Summer
HOW TO GROW Sow seeds in spring in containers or in garden in full or filtered sun; needs rich, porous soil and periodic fertilizing. No water in late summer. Thrives in rock gardens and woodlands.
CULTIVARS AND RELATED SPECIES Many dwarf *Delphinium* selections are available, with no staking necessary: *D. grandiflorum* 'Blue Butterfly' is only 12 to 18 inches tall; Zones 3 to 8.

Epilobium canum subsp. *latifolia* (formerly *Zauschneria californica* subsp. *latifolia*)
CALIFORNIA FUCHSIA, HUMMINGBIRD FUCHSIA
NATIVE HABITAT Dry slopes and ridges of California foothills
GROWTH TYPE Herbaceous perennial; low-growing, multibranched
HARDINESS ZONES 8 to 10
FLOWER COLOR Bright red or red-orange, long, tubular flowers 1 to $1^{1}/_{2}$ inches long with projecting stamens growing at ends of upright or arching stems. Hummers can't resist this one! If you have to choose just one plant, this should be it.
HEIGHT 4 to 20 inches
BLOOMING PERIOD Summer and fall
HOW TO GROW Drought-tolerant groundcover; thrives in hot, dry summers. Will spread throughout the garden by roots and by reseeding itself. Groom in winter or it will become twiggy.
CULTIVARS AND RELATED SPECIES Most California fuchsias are red-flowered, but 'Solidarity Pink' produces flesh-pink tubular blossoms on 10- to 12-inch stems.

Right: *Epilobium canum*
subsp. *latifolia*

PACIFIC COAST

Iochroma cyaneum

Galvezia speciosa
ISLAND BUSH
SNAPDRAGON

NATIVE HABITAT Santa Catalina, San Clemente, and Guadalupe Islands off the Pacific Coast of North America
GROWTH TYPE Perennial shrub that can climb or sprawl on other shrubs
HARDINESS ZONES 9 to 10
FLOWER COLOR Rose-red, tubular, 1-inch miniature snapdragon flowers clustered around tips of branches
HEIGHT 3 to 5 feet, sprawling to the same width

BLOOMING PERIOD Spring, but intermittent all year
HOW TO GROW Sun or light shade; sandy to rocky, well-drained soils. Sensitive to heavy frost. Control sprawling with winter pruning.
CULTIVARS AND RELATED SPECIES 'Firecracker' is a cultivated form that is more compact with bright red flowers.

Iochroma cyaneum
IOCHROMA

NATIVE HABITAT Tropical Central and South America
GROWTH TYPE Herbaceous perennial
HARDINESS ZONES 6 to 10
FLOWER COLOR Light blue tubular, trumpetlike flowers up to $2^{1/2}$ inches in length, clustered at terminal ends of branches
HEIGHT Stalks to 6 feet
BLOOMING PERIOD Fall
HOW TO GROW Full to partial sun to shade in well-drained soil. It is sensitive to frost and winter cover is recommended; however, if it dies back, new growth will rise from hardy roots; it will also grow from rooted cuttings.
CULTIVARS AND RELATED SPECIES The foliage and shape of *Iochroma* resemble several species of fuchsia in appearance. Many fuchsias, such as 'Gardenmeister Bonstedt', have branches terminating in large

Justicia spicigera

clusters of long, red trumpetlike flowers 2 inches long. *Fuchsia* 'China House' has individual flowers in multiple shades of pink protruding from down-swept branches.

Justicia spicigera
MEXICAN HONEYSUCKLE

NATIVE HABITAT Mexico and Central America
GROWTH TYPE Perennial shrub
HARDINESS ZONES 9 to 10
FLOWER COLOR Orange whorls of 1$^1/_2$-inch tubular flowers at tips of protruding branches
HEIGHT 6 to 8 feet
BLOOMING PERIOD All year

HOW TO GROW Full sun or light shade in sandy or loamy fertile soils. Drought tolerant; no water needed during dry season.

CULTIVARS AND RELATED SPECIES *J. brandegeana*, also known as shrimp plant, is an evergreen shrub with 3-inch spikes of white tubular flowers protruding from coppery-bronze, overlapping bracts. It blooms all year but is sensitive to frost and requires regular watering. *J. californica*, chuparosa or California belperone, is a deciduous, gray-green, low spreading shrub 2 to 5 feet high with spring blooms of bright red, clustered flowers. It needs no dry-season

PACIFIC COAST

Lupinus arcticus

have to choose just one plant, this should be it.

HEIGHT 4 to 20 inches

BLOOMING PERIOD Summer and fall

HOW TO GROW Drought tolerant groundcover; thrives in hot, dry summers. Will spread throughout the garden by roots and by reseeding itself. Groom in winter or it will become twiggy.

CULTIVARS AND RELATED SPECIES Most California fuchsias are red-flowered, but 'Solidarity Pink' produces flesh-pink tubular blossoms on 10-to 12-inch stems.

Galvezia speciosa
ISLAND BUSH SNAPDRAGON

NATIVE HABITAT Santa Catalina, San Clemente, and Guadalupe Islands off the Pacific Coast of North America

GROWTH TYPE Perennial shrub that can climb or sprawl on other shrubs

HARDINESS ZONES 9 to 10

FLOWER COLOR Rose-red, tubular, 1-inch miniature snapdragon flowers clustered around tips of branches

HEIGHT 3 to 5 feet, sprawling to the same width

BLOOMING PERIOD Spring, but intermittent all year

HOW TO GROW Sun or light shade; sandy to rocky, well-drained soils. Sensitive to heavy frost. Control sprawling with winter pruning.

CULTIVARS AND RELATED SPECIES 'Firecracker' is a cultivated form that is more compact with bright red flowers.

Iochroma cyaneum
IOCHROMA

NATIVE HABITAT Tropical Central and South America

GROWTH TYPE Herbaceous perennial

HARDINESS ZONES 6 to 10

two below joined as a keel) clustered at ends of short branches
HEIGHT Ranges from flat ground cover of 3 to 4 inches to bushes of 2 to 5 feet. Most species range from 6 to 18 inches in height.
BLOOMING PERIOD Spring, summer, and fall
HOW TO GROW Most lupines thrive in dry, sunny areas with well-drained soils. A few, such as the bush lupines, tolerate filtered shade and some dampness.
CULTIVARS AND RELATED SPECIES More than 80 species are native to California, Oregon, Washington, and Alaska. *L. breweri*, brewer lupine, grows to 9 inches in gray-green leafy mats; dense 2-inch clusters of flowers with blue banners and white centers; summer blooming; thrives on dry, stony slopes. *L. albifrons*, bush lupine, features leaves that are silvery and silky; spring flower clusters 3 to 12 inches long and flower petals of blue to red-purple; banner white- or yellow-centered; sun or shade. *L. nootkantensis* and *L. arcticus* attract Rufous Hummingbirds in southeastern Alaska.

Madronella macrantha
SCARLET MONARDELLA
NATIVE HABITAT Dry slopes of the western U.S.
GROWTH TYPE Deciduous shrub

Mimulus aurantiacus (see page 94)

HARDINESS ZONES 7 to 9
FLOWER COLOR Large, red-orange whorls of flowers with purplish bracts, irresistible to hummingbirds
HEIGHT 2 to 3 feet
BLOOMING PERIOD Mid- to late summer
HOW TO GROW Full sun; requires very well-drained soils, otherwise difficult to grow; tolerates sandy or rocky conditions. It is a good plant for the rock garden and does well in a container when gravel is added to the soil mix.

PACIFIC COAST

Mimulus cardinalis

HOW TO GROW Drought resistant but needs occasional water and some pruning to preserve lush, bright green foliage and to prevent plant from becoming woody.

CULTIVARS AND RELATED SPECIES *M. longiflorus*, southern bush monkeyflower, is similar to *M. aurantiacus*, but with larger flowers of pinkish yellow; native to Southern California. *M. puniceus*, red bush monkeyflower, has flowers similar to other monkeyflowers in all hues of red to orange.

Mimulus cardinalis
MONKEYFLOWER

NATIVE HABITAT Along streams and in moist places throughout the western U.S.

GROWTH TYPE Herbaceous perennial often grown as an annual

HARDINESS ZONES 7 to 9

FLOWER COLOR Bright orange-red, 1-inch flowers with a funnel form that widen to lobed upper and lower lips, often described as resembling a monkey face

HEIGHT 1 to 3 feet

BLOOMING PERIOD Spring and summer

HOW TO GROW Full sun or partial shade and damp conditions

CULTIVARS AND RELATED SPECIES *M. guttatus*, yellow monkeyflower, is also an inhabitant of streamside or moist locations; spreading

Mimulus aurantiacus
STICKY MONKEYFLOWER, BUSH MONKEYFLOWER

NATIVE HABITAT Coastal sage scrub and foothills throughout California

GROWTH TYPE Perennial shrub

HARDINESS ZONES 9 to 10

FLOWER COLOR Usually orange, but range from red to pink and yellow. The inch-long flowers are funnel shaped, widening to lobed upper and lower lips. Generally one flower per leaf at end of stem.

HEIGHT 4 feet

BLOOMING PERIOD Spring, summer, and fall

foliage to about 1 foot with yellow flowers resembling *M. cardinalis*.

Penstemon hartweggi and hybrids
FIREBIRD PENSTEMON

NATIVE HABITAT Most pentemons are native to the western U.S. and Mexico and thrive in varied habitats.

GROWTH TYPE Herbaceous shrubby perennial

HARDINESS ZONES 8 to 10

FLOWER COLOR Deep crimson, inch-long tubular flowers with deeply lobed upper lip; flowers clustered along but mostly near the ends of many erect stems

HEIGHT 2 to $2^{1}/_{2}$ feet

BLOOMING PERIOD Spring and summer; into fall if pruned after each bloom

HOW TO GROW Full sun or partial shade and well-drained sandy or loamy soils; thrives with periodic watering but subject to root rot in persistently damp soils.

CULTIVARS AND RELATED SPECIES Several named cultivars are readily available in nurseries. 'Apple Blossom' (sometimes called 'Huntington Pink') has pink flowers and grows to 3 feet; 'Lady Hindley' has lavender flowers; 'Garnet' is dark red; and 'Sour Grapes' has purple blossoms. Many species of penstemon are

Penstemon 'Sour Grapes'

important plants for hummingbirds and moths. All have tubular flowers that range in color from red and pinkish hues to purple to true blue. Some other popular species include *P. cardinalis*, beardtongue, which is similar to firebird penstemon but with flowers more red than deep crimson; *P. campanulatus*, bellflower beardtongue; *P. labrosus*, San Gabriel beardtongue, *P. clevelandii*, Cleveland's beardtongue; and *P. barbatus* (scarlet bugler or goldenbeard penstemon) 'Prairie Fire', and 'Elfin Pink'.

Ribes sanguineum

Rehmannia elata
REHMANNIA, CHINESE FOXGLOVE

NATIVE HABITAT China
GROWTH TYPE Herbaceous perennial
HARDINESS ZONES 6 to 9
FLOWER COLOR Foxglove-like flowers range from rose to purple with red-dotted yellow throats.
HEIGHT 2 to 3 feet
BLOOMING PERIOD Long blooming period from April through November
HOW TO GROW This species is easy to grow and spreads from underground roots; plant in rich soil. Will grow in sun but thrives with some shade. It is deciduous in colder climates, but elsewhere the basel rosette usually remains green year-round.
CULTIVARS AND RELATED SPECIES *R. glutinosa* differs from *R. elata* in having glandular hairs on its leaves.

Ribes sanguineum
FLOWERING CURRANT

NATIVE HABITAT Foothills and forested mountain slopes of western mountains to about 6,000 feet, generally in moist or damp areas
GROWTH TYPE Deciduous shrub
HARDINESS ZONES 6 to 8
FLOWER COLOR Hanging clusters of red tubular flowers
HEIGHT About 6 feet high and wide
BLOOMING PERIOD Spring
HOW TO GROW Hardy and easily adaptable to a variety of settings; often used as an ornamental in formal gardens. Prefers well-drained soil and full sun but will grow in semishade for part of the day. The slender stems can be pruned into a dense hedge.
CULTIVARS AND RELATED SPECIES There are many species of native currants and gooseberries, all with red or red and white flowers. *R. malvaceum*, pink-flowering or chaparral currant, has hanging clusters of bright pink and white

Salvia clevelandii

flowers that bloom in early spring; it requires no water once established. *R. speciosum*, fuchsia-flowered gooseberry, is an evergreen shrub with drooping, deep crimson to cherry-red flowers resembling common varieties of fuchsia; it blooms in winter and spring; it prefers sun to light shade and tolerates drought but will lose leaves in summer if not watered.

Salvia clevelandii
CLEVELAND'S SAGE
NATIVE HABITAT Chaparral and coastal sage scrub of San Diego County, California

GROWTH TYPE Evergreen shrub
HARDINESS ZONES 9 to 10
FLOWER COLOR Clusters of blue, fragrant flowers
HEIGHT To 4 feet
BLOOMING PERIOD Spring through summer
HOW TO GROW Full sun in well-drained soil. Drought tolerant; needs very little water in summer
CULTIVARS AND RELATED SPECIES Many species of sage attract hummingbirds and thrive in the arid West. Two good ones are *S. leucantha*, Mexican bush sage, with small white flowers extending from purple calyces; and *S.* 'Allen Chickering', which is lavender.

PACIFIC COAST

Salvia elegans

CULTIVARS AND RELATED SPECIES
S. splendens, scarlet sage, is an annual, sturdy plant that grows 1 to 3 feet tall, topped with dense spikes of scarlet-red flowers blooming summer and fall. *S. spathacea*, hummingbird sage, a robust perennial, has large aromatic leaves and whorls of magenta flowers. It grows best in full or filtered sun with some water. Many species of sage attract hummingbirds, and their variety in height, shape, and flower color make it easy to find plants to fit anywhere in the garden and complement any palette.

Salvia elegans
PINEAPPLE SAGE, RED SAGE

NATIVE HABITAT Mexico and Guatemala
GROWTH TYPE Perennial herb
HARDINESS ZONES 5 to 10
FLOWER COLOR Scarlet-red slender, tubular flowers
HEIGHT To 5 feet tall and wide
BLOOMING PERIOD Spring to fall, depending upon climate
HOW TO GROW Full sun or partial shade, well-drained soils; sensitive to frost. Can be grown from cuttings; prune regularly.

Silene californica
CALIFORNIA INDIAN PINK

NATIVE HABITAT California and southern Oregon foothills
GROWTH TYPE Herbaceous perennial, sometimes treated as annual
HARDINESS ZONES 8 to 10
FLOWER COLOR Flowers are vermilion, $1^{1}/_{4}$-inch wide, and fringed.
HEIGHT 6 to 16 inches
BLOOMING PERIOD Spring
HOW TO GROW Can be grown from seed. Prefers filtered shade; requires well-drained soil that is allowed to dry in summer. Can be grown in hanging baskets.
CULTIVARS AND RELATED SPECIES
Silene virginica, fire pink, native to central and eastern U.S., has red and pink selections; Zones 4 to 8.

More Hummingbird Plants for the Pacific Coast

SHRUBS

Archtostaphylos species MANZANITA Evergreen shrubs ranging from tall shrubs to prostrate groundcover, all with red bark and white, waxy, bell-shaped flowers; Zones 5 to 10, depending on species

Grevillea 'Canberra' HUMMINGBIRD FERN Evergreen shrub native to Australia with bright green, needlelike leaves; to 8 feet with clusters of small red flowers blooming in spring; Zones 6 to 9

Nicotiana glauca and *N. alata* TREE TOBACCO *N. glauca*: shrub or small tree to 20 feet with tubular yellow flowers; *N. alata:* 2- to 3-foot shrub with tubular white flowers; Zones 7 to 9

Salvia greggii RED SAGE Erect shrub to 3 or 4 feet; red (sometimes other colors) flowers late spring through fall; Zones 6 to 10

VINES

Abutilon × *hybridum* CHINESE LANTERN Broad, maplelike leaves; drooping bell-like flowers in red, pink, and yellow; Zones 6 to 9

Campsis radicans TRUMPET CREEPER Deciduous vine with large orange or red flaring tubular flowers; Zones 5 to 9

Tecomaria capensis CAPE HONEYSUCKLE Climbing vine with yellow and white fragrant flowers; native to South Africa; Zones 6 to 9

PERENNIALS AND ANNUALS

Dicentra spectabilis BLEEDING HEART Graceful but short-lived perennial with fernlike foliage and rows of small, heart-shaped, pink, rose, or white flowers on leafless stems; Zones 6 to 9

Ipomopsis aggregata SCARLET GILIA Narrow, erect single stems to 2$\frac{1}{2}$ feet with striking tubular, fanning red flowers in long, narrow clusters; Zones 4 to 7

Kniphofia uvaria RED HOT POKER Spikes of orange and yellow flowers on stems to 3 feet tall; native to South Africa; Zones 5 to 9

Monarda didyma BEE BALM Bushy perennial with long, aromatic leaves and clusters of scarlet flowers; Zones 4 to 9

Scrophularia californica BEE PLANT Large perennial with tall stalks of tiny maroon flowers; Zones 7 to 9

PACIFIC COAST

Further Reading

Armitage's Native Plants for North American Gardens
Allan M. Armitage
Timber Press, 2006

Attracting Birds to Southern Gardens
Thomas Pope, Neil Odenwald, and Charles Fryling Jr.
Taylor Publishing 1993

Attracting Butterflies & Hummingbirds to Your Backyard
Sally Roth
Rodale Books, 2002

The Audubon Society Bird Garden
Stephen W. Kress
Dorling Kindersley, 1995

The Audubon Society Guide to Attracting Birds
Stephen W. Kress
Cornell University Press, 2006

Bird-by-Bird Gardening
Sally Roth
Rodale Books, 2006

Bird Gardens
Stephen W. Kress (ed.)
Brooklyn Botanic Garden, 1998

A Field Guide to Hummingbirds of North America (Peterson Field Guides)
Sheri Williamson
Houghton Mifflin, 2002

Gardening with Native Plants of the South
Sally and Andy Wasowski
Taylor Publishing, 1994

Hummingbird Gardens
Nancy L. Newfield and Barbara Nielson
Houghton Mifflin, 1996

Hummingbirds of the American West
Lynn Hassler Kaufman
Rio Nuevo Publishers, 2002

The Hummingbirds of North America
Paul A. Johnsgard
Smithsonian Institution Press, 1997

Songbirds in Your Garden
John K. Terres
Algonquin Books, 1994

Stokes Hummingbird Book
Donald and Lillian Stokes
Little, Brown and Co., 1989

Organizations

For further information about attracting hummingbirds and other backyard wildlife, contact the following groups:

Cornell Laboratory of Ornithology
159 Sapsucker Woods Road
Ithaca, NY 14850
www.birds.cornell.edu

The Hummingbird Society
6560 Highway 179
Sedona, AZ 86351
www.hummingbirdsociety.org

National Audubon Society
700 Broadway
New York, NY 10003
www.audubon.org

National Wildlife Federation
11100 Wildlife Center Drive
Reston, VA 20190
www.nwf.org

Nursery Sources

NORTHEAST AND MIDWEST

Bergeson Nursery
4177 County Highway 1
Fertile, MN 56540
218-945-6988
www.bergesonnursery.com
No mail order

Kurt Bluemel, Inc.
2740 Greene Lane
Baldwin, MD 21013
800-498-1560
www.kurtbluemel.com

Carroll Gardens, Inc.
444 East Main Street
Westminster, MD 21157-5540
800-638-6334
www.carrollgardens.com

**Wild Earth Native
Plant Nursery**
P.O. Box 7258
Freehold, NJ 07728
732-308-9777
wildearthnpn@compuserv.com
$2 catalog

SOUTHEAST

Apalachee Native Nursery
Route 3, Box 156
Monticello, FL 32344
850-997-8976
apalnative@aol.com

**Green Images Native
Landscape Plants**
1333 Taylor Creek Road
Christmas, FL 32709
407-568-1333
greenimages@aol.com

SOUTHWEST

Great Basin Natives
Box 114
Holden, UT 84636
435-795-2303
www.greatbasinnatives.com

High Country Gardens
2902 Rufina Street
Santa Fe, NM 87507
800-925-9387
www.high

**Living Stones Nursery
Plants for the Southwest**
2936 N. Stone Avenue
Tucson, AZ 85705
520-628-8773
www.lithops.net

Wild Seed
P.O. Box 27751
Tempe, AZ 85042-4718
602-276-3536
Free catalog

PACIFIC COAST
California Flora Nursery
P.O. Box 3
Fulton, CA 95439
707-528-8813
No mail order
www.calfloranursery.com

Cornflower Farms
P.O. Box 896
Elk Grove, CA 95759
916-689-1015
www.cornflowerfarms.com

Forestfarm
990 Tetherow Road
Williams, OR 97544
541-846-7269
www.forestfarm.com

SOURCE DIRECTORIES
Andersen Horticultural Library
Source List of Plants and Seeds
Minnesota Landscape Arboretum
Box 39
Chaska, MN 55318-1613
952-443-1405
www.arboretum.umn.edu/library/

Association of Florida
Native Nurseries
877-352-2366
www.afnn.org

California Native Plant Society
2707 K Street, Suite 1
Sacramento, CA 95816-5113
916-447-2677
www.cnps.org

Hortus Northwest
P.O. Box 955
Canby, OR 97013
Native Plant Resources
for the Pacific Northwest
http://dnr.metrokc.gov/wlr/pi/
npresrcs.htm

New England
Wild Flower Society
180 Hemenway Road
Framingham, MA 01701-0269
508-877-7630
www.newfs.org

North American Native
Plant Society
P.O. Box 84, Station D
Etobikoke, ON M9A 4X1 Canada
416-631-4438
www.nonps.org

Lady Bird Johnson
Wildflower Center
4801 LaCrosse Blvd.
Austin, TX 78739
512-929-3600

Contributors

Jesse Grantham is the condor recovery coordinator for the U.S. Fish and Wildlife Service, in Ventura, California, and former executive director of the Mississippi State office of the National Audubon Society. He has extensive experience in horticulture, habitat restoration, and wildlife management. He writes and lectures throughout the country on gardening for wildlife.

Beth Huning is coordinator of the San Francisco Bay Joint Venture, which works to protect and restore habitat for birds, fish, and other wildlife. She is a former director of education for the National Audubon Society in California, where she directed the education and wildlife conservation programs and coordinated the development of habitat programs and demonstration gardens, including a model hummingbird garden.

Stephen W. Kress is vice president for bird conservation for the National Audubon Society and manager of the society's Maine coast seabird sanctuaries. He teaches ornithology classes at the Audubon Camp in Maine and for the Cornell Laboratory of Ornithology. He guest-edited the Brooklyn Botanic Garden handbook *Bird Gardens* (1998) and is also author of *The Audubon Society Guide to Attracting Birds, The Audubon Backyard Birdwatcher* (with Robert Burton), *The Audubon Society Bird Garden, The Audubon Society Birder's Handbook*, and other publications on birds and their management.

Lynn Hassler Kaufman has been bird-watching, gardening, and studying plants for more than 25 years. She is a horticultural consultant for Garden Insights, in Tucson, Arizona, and has served as vice president of the Arizona Native Plant Society and as a staff member of the Tucson Botanical Gardens. She writes widely about gardening and is also a columnist for *Bird Watcher's Digest* and author of *Hummingbirds of the American West*; she also contributed to the Kaufman Focus Guide *Birds of North America*.

Credits

ALL ILLUSTRATIONS BY
Steve Buchanan

PHOTOS

A. & J. Binnis/Vireo, page 47

R. & N. Bowers/Vireo, pages 6, 9

David Cavagnaro, pages 35, 41, 42, 51 both, 54, 55, 57, 63, 65, 69, 70, 72 both, 82 top, 83, 87, 89, 90, 96, 97, 98

R. & S. Day/Vireo, pages 10, 11, 48

Alan & Linda Detrick, pages 53, 56

C.A. Fogle/Vireo, page 12

Susan M. Glascock, pages 52, 60

S. Howell/Vireo, page 33 top

D. Huntington/Vireo, page 32

Charles Mann, pages 43, 44, 62, 64, 72 bottom, 75, 77, 81, 85, 91, 94, 95

Charles W. Melton, cover

Jerry Pavia, pages 66, 68, 79, 92, 93

B. Randall/Vireo, page 101

S. & S. Rucker/Vireo, page 33 bottom

H.P. Smith/Vireo, pages 1, 45

T.J. Ulrich/Vireo, page 4

USDA Hardiness Zone Map

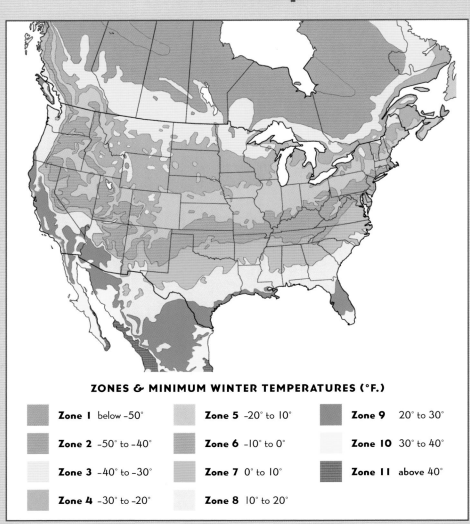

ZONES & MINIMUM WINTER TEMPERATURES (°F.)

Zone 1 below –50°	**Zone 5** –20° to 10°	**Zone 9** 20° to 30°
Zone 2 –50° to –40°	**Zone 6** –10° to 0°	**Zone 10** 30° to 40°
Zone 3 –40° to –30°	**Zone 7** 0° to 10°	**Zone 11** above 40°
Zone 4 –30° to –20°	**Zone 8** 10° to 20°	

Index

PROVIDING EXPERT GARDENING ADVICE FOR OVER 60 YEARS

Join Brooklyn Botanic Garden as an annual Subscriber Member and receive our next three gardening handbooks delivered directly to you, plus *Plants & Gardens News*, *BBG Members News*, and reciprocal privileges at many botanic gardens across the country. Visit www.bbg.org/subscribe for details.

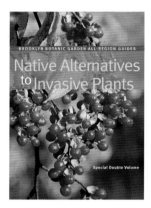

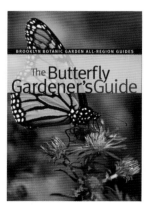

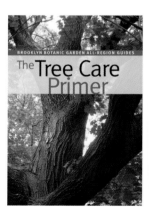

BROOKLYN BOTANIC GARDEN ALL-REGION GUIDES

World renowned for pioneering gardening information, Brooklyn Botanic Garden's award-winning guides provide practical advice in a compact format for gardeners in every region of North America. To order other fine titles, call 718-623-7286 or shop online at shop.bbg.org. For additional information about Brooklyn Botanic Garden, call 718-623-7200 or visit www.bbg.org.